Making the Connection
Learning Skills Through Literature 3-6

Also by Patricia Pavelka:

Making the Connection:
Learning Skills Through Literature (K-2)

Making the Connection
Learning Skills Through Literature (3-6)

Patricia Pavelka

Crystal Springs Books
Peterborough, New Hampshire

©1997 by Patricia Pavelka

Printed in the United States of America
01 00 99 98   6 5 4 3

Published and distributed by:
   Crystal Springs Books
   Ten Sharon Road, Box 500
   Peterborough, NH 03458-0500
   1-800-321-0401

Publisher Cataloging-in-Publication Data

Pavelka, Patricia, 1959-
        Making the connection : learning skills through literature (3-6) / Patricia
Pavelka ; [illustrated by Phyllis Pittet].—1st ed.
[144] p. : ill ; cm.
Includes bibliography and index.
Contents: Part I. Teaching through meaningful contexts, creating a print-rich environment and
components of a process classroom, and teaching to students' needs. — Part II. Techniques to
advance comprehension and vocabulary development. — Part III. Examples of how to teach
specific skills to students in grades 3 through 6. — Part IV. Ways to accommodate for different
abilities in the classroom.
ISBN 1-884548-11-3
1. Reading (Elementary)—Language experience approach. 2. Language experience approach in
education. 3. Language arts (Elementary). I. Pittet, Phyllis, ill. II. Title.
371.6 / 4044—dc20   1996   CIP
LC Card Number : 95-71328

Publishing Manager: Lorraine Walker
Editor: Aldene Fredenburg
Book Design: Susan Dunholter
Cover and Book Illustrations: Phyllis Pittet
Production Coordinator: Christine Landry

Woodworking Consultants: Earl Medeiros
                         Tim Hopkins

The verse from *The Great Gray Owl*, by Orin Cochrane, which appears on page 79, is reprinted by permission
of the author.

Dedicated to:

The Reverend Peter Vanderveen
and
The Family of Saint Ann's

Acknowledgments

Thank you to Richard LaPorta, my brother, for his endless hours of assisting, revising, and encouragement; Earl Medeiros, for building our classroom libraries; Aldene Fredenburg, for her editing expertise; Lorraine Walker for her continued vision; The Society For Developmental Education family for their constant support and help; and especially to my mentor, Jim Grant.

Table of Contents

INTRODUCTION
Why Literature?

This second volume of *Making the Connection: Learning Skills Through Literature* is geared for grades 3-6. The first book was geared for grades K-2.

These books were written after spending many years working within the constraints of a basal series. My classroom from year to year had a wealth of "paperwork" available to students: workbooks, reproducibles, blackline masters, dittos, etc. These were the materials I thought necessary for students to use in order for them to learn skills. Skills were taught in isolation, and were completely unrelated to the process of reading. My older classrooms were especially over-flowing with these items, because many students could work independently. They completed a multitude of independent work such as:

- filling in the blanks
- looking up multitudes of words in the dictionary and copying down the definitions
- answering 5-10 literal questions about the reading assignment
- ETC!

My students were passive participants in the reading process, and their attitude and achievement reflected that.

I started moving away from commercial programs towards children's literature. However, I was concerned about skills. How was I, as a teacher, going to make sure I was accountable for the skills I needed to teach at my grade level if there was no basal program to follow? How were the students going to learn the skills if they didn't have workbooks to practice them in?

The first thing I needed to do was to find books that were good models for teaching specific reading and writing skills. At first this seemed like an overwhelming task; but I took each skill one at a time. For example, when I was going to do a lesson on adjectives, I began looking for books and poems that used adjectives abundantly. We discussed what adjectives were and the skill of using adjectives in writing to make students' pieces come alive. We also looked at many examples of how they were being used in meaningful contexts, rather than just putting isolated sentences on the board.

The next step was to think about what students could do instead of completing numerous workbook pages and dittos. In the past, my students completed two workbook pages where they had to read sentences and circle the adjectives, and then did two dittos where they had to fill in the blanks with adjectives listed at the top of the pages.

Students were now going through the books they were reading and picking out adjectives that described their characters. They were writing down adjectives that described the setting of their book. My students also wrote adjectives to describe themselves and each other. They were actively involved in the learning process, rather than being passively involved. Assignments started to become more meaningful to students instead of just isolated practice.

For one activity, I had each student bring in an object from home. We placed each of the objects in separate bags and put the bags in a pile on the floor. Each student picked a bag and secretly wrote adjectives to describe what was in it. Later, we met on the carpet and placed all the objects on the floor so everyone could see them. While one student read his or her list of adjectives, we all tried to figure out which object was being described.

Students as Independent Readers

Most students in grades three to six recognize many words on sight and can apply different word identification strategies. Many are reading a variety of materials independently. The focus for these students is more on the interpretation and understanding of the text, rather than the act of reading it.

Let's look at the characteristics of independent readers and writers, as well as the characteristics of the reading materials.

Independent readers and writers:

- recognize the majority of words at sight
- read with fluency
- use the three cueing systems simultaneously
- self-correct to gain meaning
- adjust the meanings of words depending upon the context in which they are used
- read and write independently
- make inferences
- draw conclusions
- read to learn (informational books)
- fully understand story elements
- begin to rely on visual cues for spelling rather than auditory cues
- can write using a variety of different forms
- read a wide range of different genres

Characteristics of Independent Reading Materials

- illustrations are at a minimum
- vocabulary becomes increasingly challenging
- children need to infer meaning from the story
- more characters are introduced and developed
- story elements are more fully developed
- language challenges are introduced (metaphors, similes)
- chapters appear

Making the Connection: Learning Skills Through Literature (3-6) reflects the change in students' reading development in these upper grades. In this second volume, I have added a new section on comprehension and vocabulary, as well as more information which will help students with the general skills of interpreting and analyzing texts.

In Part I, *Teaching Through Meaningful Contexts,* I begin by looking at how to set up the classroom environment so that reading and writing are shown to be the priority. This part also explains in detail how to use a planning guide. As I began coordinating specific skills with literature, I needed a place to organize the information, and created the planning guide to help with this organization.

Part I looks at specific strategies that can be used to reinforce skills students have learned throughout the year. It gives specific suggestions about how to support those who need it, and to challenge those who are ready to go further.

Part II, *Comprehension and Vocabulary*, discusses two areas that play a key role in the reading program for third- through sixth-grade students. Students are no longer learning to read, but reading to learn. This part gives a wealth of specific ideas and activities that can be used to support and enrich vocabulary development and comprehension.

Part III, *Teaching Skills Through Literature,* is a compilation of the planning sheets I created. Skills appear in alphabetical order.

Although very specific skills are given, along with books and activities that can be used, they are not meant to be "written in stone." They were developed based on the curriculum requirements and the specific needs of my students. Many of them may be appropriate for you, but it is also important for you to be able to develop the integration between skills and literature based on your students' needs and your school's curriculum. That is where the planning guide will be most helpful.

Part IV, *Including the Struggling Learner,* provides ideas and strategies for managing classrooms that have students who are working at various levels of ability. This part explores how to organize and use flexible grouping, and gives resources for less proficient readers.

As teachers use the ideas presented here, they will begin to see a change in students' motivation, interest, and achievement, while feeling confident that they are effectively teaching the skills their curriculum demands. The difference between my worksheet/ditto/blackline master approach of the past and my present, literature-based approach, is evident as shown in the chart on page 4.

CHARACTERISTICS OF STUDENTS

THEN	NOW
unmotivated	motivated
uninterested	interested
saw little meaning in reading and writing	see reading and writing as a means of communicating and a form of enjoyment
could not transfer skills	apply skills in meaningful contexts
were schooltime readers	are readers in and out of school
unsure	confident, high self-esteem
not risk takers	risk takers
majority of time spent on paperwork	majority of time spent on reading
did not talk about or share books	constantly sharing and borrowing books from each other

CHARACTERISTICS OF MATERIALS

THEN	NOW
uninteresting	interesting
skills taught in isolation	skills taught in meaningful contexts
contrived language	predictable, natural language
meaning was not a priority	meaning dominates
phonics and skills were the heart of the program	comprehension and meaning are the heart of the program
levels	no levels
dull illustrations	beautiful illustrations
enormous amounts of paperwork	meaningful extensions
story elements kept to a minimum	story elements fully developed

From *Making the Connection: Learning Skills Through Literature (K-2)*

Part I
Teaching Through
Meaningful Contexts

Creating a Print-rich Environment

How do you create a print-rich environment in the upper grades? Is it important? These were questions I had when I moved from teaching kindergarten to fourth grade. If creating that kind of environment is important with young children, shouldn't it be equally important to upper elementary students?

Children learn more by what we do than what we say. It's like that old saying: Practice what you preach. If we are *telling* our students that reading and writing are important, that we place a high value on these two issues, then we also have to *show* them, at all grade levels!

We do this by surrounding children with print. In the fourth-grade classroom pictured below, for instance, all of Roahl Dahl's books are available for students to read. Literature extension activities provide children with the opportunity to work, either individually or in groups, on their literacy. The current science theme is supported by the presence of ocean-related books and magazines (shown here on the floor beneath the bulletin board). The classroom includes a corner library (to the left of the bulletin board). The library is shown in detail on page 8.

Classroom Libraries

Libraries need to be inviting, cozy places for students to be. Display books prominently in a variety of ways. Displaying books with the front cover showing will be more inviting to students than just keeping them in bookshelves with the spines out. Feature different books each week or every other week.

Use rugs, cushions, pillows, bean bag chairs, couches, and oversized chairs, to provide comfortable places for students to settle.

It is important to display books at many different reading levels to accommodate the range of reading abilities in the classroom. There must be books easy enough for all children to read, so that they can feel successful and confident. A variety of reading materials should be available — fiction, nonfiction, magazines, joke books, newspapers, books written by students, etc. When libraries and books are the focus of the classroom, students see that teachers value reading.

Reading should *be* the work, not what is done when the work is completed!

Creating Shelves for Your Classroom

Trying to get enough bookcases and bookshelves to display books can be difficult. The pictures below and on the previous pages show what can be done to create libraries where books are prominently displayed, cover out, without being very costly. Earl Medeiros designed and built these shelves.

Materials

1 piece of 1" x 6" x [length of your bookshelf] wooden board per shelf
1 piece of 1" x 4" x [desired height; see illustration] for each wall bracket support.
    (You need at least two, but should have a wall bracket support every 32 inches.)
wood glue
nails (2-inch finish nails are good)
screws and anchors to fasten bracket supports to wall; will differ depending on composition of wall

Instructions

From each 1" x 6" board, cut:
    two strips $1^3/_8$" wide
    one strip $2^3/_8$" wide

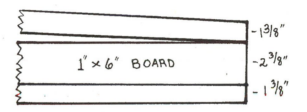

Glue and nail one strip of $1^3/_8$" board to the edge of the $2^3/_8$" piece, and the other $1^3/_8$" strip to the top of the $2^3/_8$" piece.

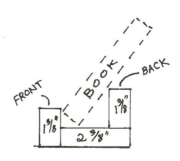

Nail or screw the 1" x 4" wall bracket supports to the backs of the shelves. The distance between shelves is determined by the height of the books.

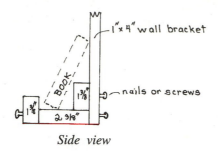

Side view

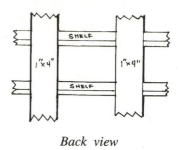

Back view

Screw the supports into the wall.

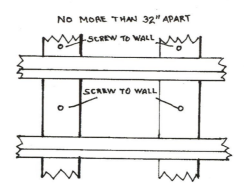

Components of a Process Classroom

Reading Aloud

The book, *Becoming a Nation of Readers: The Report of the Commission on Reading*, states,

> The single most important activity for building the knowledge required for eventual success in reading is reading aloud to children.

This quote depicts the importance of reading aloud to our younger students to help them develop into successful readers. But reading aloud is equally important to our older students. In her book, *In the Middle: Writing, Reading, and Learning with Adolescents*, Nancie Atwell states,

> Read-alouds led many kids to borrow the books I shared and to look for other works by those authors, to go beyond listening to a more active and personal involvement with texts.

The more students read, the better readers they become. So we need to get students excited and motivated to read. One of our goals for students is to foster a love of reading and writing. Reading aloud is what hooks my students on books. I read aloud from a wide range of materials and genres which includes:

Fiction

Nonfiction

Poems

Magazines

Students' own writing

Comic books

Short stories

Newspapers

Picture books

Fairy tales/traditional literature

If we are reading something and find we are really not enjoying it, we stop! We make sure we have given it a fair chance, and then we analyze why we were not interested in the text and go on from there.

Jim Trelease, author of *The Read-Aloud Handbook* and *The New Read-Aloud Handbook,* states that "Reading aloud is the best advertisement because it works." Reading aloud:

- Enhances vocabulary development
- Models skillful oral reading
- Creates lifetime readers, not just schooltime readers
- Creates a positive attitude toward reading
- Motivates children to read
- Improves listening comprehension
- Stimulates the imagination

- Establishes the reading/writing connection
- Enriches and increases students' knowledge
- Incites thought-provoking discussions
- Allows us to study and explore different literary devices

Reading aloud is a great catalyst for writing. I was reading *Half-A-Moon Inn,* by Paul Fleischman, to my class. I stopped at an exciting part one morning, and we were going to continue reading in the afternoon. During the language arts block in the morning one of my struggling students decided to write a prediction about what was going to happen when we began reading in the afternoon. This was a child who was not interested in books because he had difficulties reading and writing. Yet he was so motivated by the read-aloud, he couldn't stand waiting until the afternoon. He needed to write about the book. Here is his piece.

> I Thingk Aaron IS goingr to get cot BY MISS. Grackie. and I thingk the Rag men iS going TO Save Aaron. thch Lourd tom IS going to cum out of th cellar an TheiRag man and Aaron are going to go to the Police. then Lord tom and miss. Grackie are gowing toget arrested and go to prison. and Aaron and the rag men are going to get Lost and Aaron iS going to FinD HiS motha

[I think Aaron is going to get caught by Miss Grackle. I think the Ragman is going to save Aaron. Then Lord Tom is going to come out of the cellar. Then Ragman and Aaron are going to go to the police. Then Lord Tom and Miss Grackle are going to get arrested and go to prison. Aaron and the Ragman are going to get lost and Aaron is going to find his mother.]

Sustained Silent Reading

"The amount of time children spend reading silently in school is associated with year-to-year gains in reading achievement." (Allington 1984)

"Sustained silent reading time must not be viewed as an optional enrichment activity; it should be treated as an integral part of the reading curriculum. Only through generous allotments of time for reading will students acquire the motivation, fluency, and breadth of experience necessary for becoming life-long readers." (O'Donnell and Wood 1992)

These are some guidelines we have established as a classroom for Sustained Silent Reading (SSR):

- Students select their own book(s).
- We put a sign on the door so there are no interruptions.
- Students may read anywhere in the classroom.
- The teacher also reads.

Using a Planning Guide

I created and designed this planning guide to help organize my thoughts and ideas. It let me see what books were good models for certain skills and what activities and literature extensions could be done. I kept these planning guides in a notebook, with the skills listed in alphabetical order. This made it easier for me to find a certain skill quickly when I added to it.

The more you work with this planning guide, the more manageable and easier it becomes. Many times I would not be thinking about trying to find a certain poem or book for a skill — it just happened. I'd be looking at some poems or pick up a new book to read, and the skills just jumped out at me. I would go back to my planning guides and add the new resource.

The planning guide is divided into three sections:

Book

This is where I list the book and/or poem that is a good model of certain skills.

Skills

This is where I list the skill(s) we are working on when using the literature. Many times certain resources (books, poems, etc.) are excellent models for a number of different skills. When that happens I make a separate planning sheet for each skill that is appropriate and add the sheets alphabetically to my notebook.

Activities and Literature Extensions

What activities will you be doing to help students acquire the skill(s) you are working on? I usually do these in a whole-group or small-group format.

What kinds of extensions can students do to extend and enrich their interaction with the book and the skill? Most of the extensions are done independently. (I usually have students do some kind of writing activity.)

How to use the planning guide

On the following page you will find an example of a completed planning guide. You can fill out the planning guide in one of two ways:

1. Choose a book you like and then find a skill that is embedded in the text, or
2. Choose the skill you want to introduce and then find books and poems that contain the skill used in a meaningful context.

I use both approaches in filling out the guides. For example, the book, *My Side of the Mountain*, by Jean Craighead George, is one of my favorites. So I wrote down the name of the book first and then proceeded to look for any skills that I could address while using the book. (See page 14.) Another time, I knew I wanted to work on comparing and contrasting with my students. So I chose that skill first and then looked for books that would be good to compare and contrast (see page 15). A blank planning guide page is provided for your use on page 16.

Use Quality Literature as the Heart of Your Skills Instruction.

Book	My Side of the Mountain	**1**

Skills | **2**

Similes

Activities and Literature Extensions | **3**

keep track of similes while reading

make simile books from story

create personal simile books

make one of Sam's 'inventions'

add an incident; What would Sam write?

1 (Book)

This is a favorite book of mine. My students really enjoy reading it. The first thing I did was write down the name of the book.

2 (Skills)

After choosing the book, *My Side of the Mountain*, I looked for skills that the book addresses in its text. This book contains many similes, so that is the skill I chose. Similes are also a part of our curriculum at the fourth- and fifth-grade levels.

3 (Activities and Literature Extensions)

These are some activities and extensions that can be done to reinforce the skill using the literature.

Use Quality Literature as the Heart of Your Skills Instruction.

Book: Cinderella

Princess Furball, The Egyptian Cinderella, Yeh-Shen, Mufaro's Beautiful Daughter, Rough-Faced Girl

1

Skills

Comparing and Contrasting

3

Activities and Literature Extensions

Venn diagrams

graphs and charts for comparing

1 (Skills)

Our curriculum had comparing and contrasting as a skill my students needed to know. The first thing I did was to write down that skill.

2 (Book)

The second thing I did was to think about books that would be good resources to use for this skill. I chose the many different versions of Cinderella.

3 (Activities and Literature Extensions)

These are some activities and extensions that can be done to reinforce the skill using the literature.

**Use Quality Literature as the Heart
of Your Skills Instruction.**

Book

Skills

**Activities and
Literature Extensions**

Strategies to Reinforce Skills and Accommodate for Different Abilities

In Part III of this book you will find a section that goes along with each skill and piece of literature called *Using Any Book.* These suggestions and activities deal with two issues:

1. varying levels of readers within our classrooms; and

2. reinforcement of skills throughout the year.

More specific information on dealing with struggling readers is included in Part IV.

Varying Levels of Readers

Within our classrooms there are students at varying levels of ability. Some can be reading significantly above grade level, and some at grade level; some may be nonreaders. Trying to accommodate each ability does seem overwhelming at times. Often at the upper primary level, students understand concepts that are introduced and taught at grade level, but then need to apply those concepts at their own reading level.

For example, when I was teaching at the fourth grade level, there was one child in the classroom reading at the primer level, some reading at a second-grade level, and some at grade level. Three were reading significantly above grade level. When we studied the skill *verbs,* most students could understand the concept of a verb, but needed to apply that concept at their independent level when working. So when an assignment was given to the class to look in the books they were reading and find examples of verbs, John was doing the activity using the book *Mr. Mitchell Brings the Mail,* an emergent-level book; Dale was using a Cam Jansen book; Caitlyn used *James and the Giant Peach*; and Jen used *Call it Courage.* When we met as a class, each child brought many samples of verbs that were found in their pieces of literature. All children could be a part of the activity, regardless of reading ability.

Reinforcement of Skills

I found myself very frustrated throughout the school year because my students were not remembering skills we had just worked on the week before, never mind something we had learned about months ago! I saw very little carryover of skills beyond the days or week we were concentrating on them.

For example: in October, when we were working on the skill of making words plurals, my students did a fantastic job on isolated skill sheets. Most achieved mastery of the skill by the end of the week it was taught. Some even applied it to their writing *that week.* But two months later, I could count on my right hand the number of students who were correctly using and spelling plurals. Most had forgotten how to apply the rules and skill. It was as if they had never been exposed to it.

In the section, *Using Any Book*, you will find ways to apply and reinforce concepts throughout the whole school year. For example, one year we had learned about adjectives and nouns in November. Every month after that, students were responsible for using the reproducibles found on pages 71, 72, and 77 to review and reinforce the concepts of adjectives and nouns; so in June, my students were still applying those concepts and skills that we had learned in September and October. They were also applying them in the context of the books they were reading, rather than on isolated skill sheets and workbook pages.

Skill Charts

Think of the number of skills your students are required to learn throughout the school year. It's no wonder that they forget to apply them weeks and/or months later. Even the students who have no difficulties learning and reading will often forget to use these skills and concepts. Some students need constant support in order to remember and apply these skills.

Using skill charts is a way of having skills and concepts available *all year* for students. Make a skill chart with your students for every skill learned throughout the whole year. Here are some charts that we made when learning about subjects and predicates, and about plurals.

It is imperative to give students an active role in making the charts. After we complete a unit on a skill, we make a chart. First, we brainstorm on the board all of the components of that skill. Next, we look at all of the information and decide how to condense, revise and organize it so that it makes sense and is usable. I do the final writing on the

---

Plurals

1. Add (s) to most nouns
   apple - apples   book - books

2. Add (es) to nouns ending in
   ch, sh, x, s
   gas - gases   patch - patches

3. When noun ends consonant y,
   change the y to (i) and add (es)
   party - parties   penny - pennies

4. When a noun ends in f or fe
   change the f, fe to (v) and add (es)

5. Some nouns completely change
   mouse - mice   child - children
   foot - feet   man - men

A sentence has 2 parts

Subject - who or what sentence is about

Predicate - what the subject is or does

The jazz (band) (played) its
favorite song.

A sea (gull) (is) about the
size of a pigeon.

Simple subject -   most important word
                   in subject

Simple predicate - verb

---

chart, so that it is big and readable, but all of the information comes directly from the students.

You can keep three to four charts up at a time, depending on your wall space. When a new skill needs to go up, the oldest one comes down. It gets put onto a chart stand with rings. The information is still available for students to refer to *all year!*

When I think about the line of students at my desk, many times their questions are about skills that we have already studied that the child forgot, or didn't apply properly. In the past, I would usually get a scrap of paper and say, "Remember when we did this . . . ?" Now when those questions come up, I can say to students, "Get the chart on [verbs] and review the information. If you still don't understand it, then come up to me with the chart."

The line at my desk has decreased dramatically. I can also hear my students say to each other, "Did you look at the chart? You know she's going to tell you to look at it or bring it up to her." Now when students come up to me, their questions are usually specific. Instead of that familiar saying, "I don't get it," they have a chart in hand and can pinpoint where the confusion is.

The first year we used skill charts I thought, "Great, now I won't have to ever make them again" . . . *wrong!* In order for students to really feel empowered and to take ownership of their own learning, they need to have an active role in making the charts. At the end of each year, I send the charts home with students and we begin again with the new class.

I also had some beautiful store-bought charts, but my students rarely used them because they didn't have any ownership in them.

Two excellent resources for students and teachers to help with skills are the books, *Write Source 2000* and *Writers INC.* Both are available through:

> Write Source
> Box 460
> Burlington, Wisconsin 53105
> 1-800-445-8613

If you use these books as resources in your classroom, add masking tape tabs to help students find information they need at their fingertips. Also, Crystal Springs Books has tabs that can be used instead of the masking tape. To order them, call 1-800-321-0401.

Modeling

As you use the ideas presented in this book, especially the reproducibles and open-ended activities, keep this in mind:

> Before asking students to do any activity independently, model it three times.

When thinking back to that constant line at my desk with students saying "I don't get it," I remember my feelings of frustration, and of never having enough time to get everything done. When I gave students their assignments or independent work to do, most of the time I just told them what to do. Yes, there were times that I did model something, but only once, and then I expected them to be able to do it on their own. And do it *well!*

Then I received a new pen and pencil set as a gift. When my pencil ran out of lead, I went to my brother Rich and asked him how to refill it. He took the pencil from me and demonstrated how to do it. I watched him and thought, I can do that. The next thing he did was to take the lead out and give me back the pencil and say, "Now you do it." Easy, I thought. I took it in my hands, looked at it and then said those four dreaded words my students always said:

"I don't get it!"

I then asked Rich to do it again so that I could watch him. After he modeled the procedure a number of times, I successfully completed the task. I immediately thought of my students and our usual scenario:

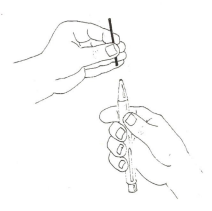

1. I would explain and/or model something once.

2. I would ask the students if everyone understood the task.

3. They would all shake their heads and say, "Uh, huh," with smiles on their faces.

4. I would give the assignment.

5. Without fail, the line began to form at my desk with students who didn't understand the assignment.

Now, when there are assignments that students will be doing throughout the whole year, such as the reproducibles and open-ended activities found in this book, I follow a format for modeling that consists of three basic steps:

First —

I put the assignment on an overhead projector and complete it as my students watch me. There is little or no student input at this time. Students watch me. As I complete the assignment I think aloud. I want students to get into my mind to see what I do to organize this specific task, and how I follow through.

Some of my students are very "task-oriented." They *go!* They do not take a moment to think about the task or to organize themselves for success. My own thinking aloud helps model that thought process to students.

Second —

I model the same assignment or task using different materials or pieces of literature. Now students begin to give me some input. We do the assignment together. I ask students to think aloud. As they give me suggestions and ideas, I want them to explain how and why they came up with them.

Third —

This time when I model the assignment I am basically my students' hands. They come up with all of the ideas and suggestions, and I write them down.

I do it.

We do it.

You do it.

Part II
Comprehension and Vocabulary Development

Comprehension

As I began leaving the basal and workbook and moved toward literature-based reading, comprehension was an area that concerned me, especially with my older students. I wanted to make sure they understood everything the chapters were saying, so I made up comprehension questions. I wrote about 6–12 questions per reading assignment, and gave them to my students every day. When I look back and analyze those questions, two things stick out in my mind:

1. Most of the questions were literal, and

2. This was the reason my students defined reading as "answering questions."

My students had been given little or no instruction in knowing how to answer questions.

One strategy I discovered to be extremely effective in helping students successfully deal with comprehension questions is called Question-Answer Relationships (QARs), developed by Pearson and Johnson (1978). QARs help students learn about the process they use to formulate answers. It helps students become aware of the different methods or information sources needed for answering different types of questions. I have seen this heightened awareness increase some of my students' abilities as they answer comprehension questions about both narrative and expository texts.

There are three basic question-answer relationships:

Literal

These are just that, literal questions. The answers are *Right There*. The answer is directly written and stated in the text (right there). The words used to make up the question are the same words that are in the answer.

*Students are actually **reading the lines.***

Interpretive

When faced with these questions, students will constantly come up to me and say, "The answer is not there." And they are right! The answer is not there in black and white. They need to make inferences in order to come up with the answer. Students need to *Think and Search* to find the answers.

*Students are actually **reading between the lines.***

Applied

These are questions that need to be answered using your own experiences. These answers are not in the book. You must find the answers *On Your Own*.

*Students are actually **reading beyond the lines.***

When I begin teaching students how to use QARs, I start with very easy materials. I ask students to tell me some of their favorite books when they were young. Usually *Goldilocks and the Three Bears* is mentioned. I take that book and make a copy of some pages and put them on the overhead. We read the page on the overhead and then I ask some *literal* (Right There) questions. I write the questions on the board so students can see that the words used to make up the question are the same ones that contain the answer. For example, this question is written on the board:

What did Mama Bear <u>pour into the bowls</u>?

We find the answer on the page and underline the same words in the question and answer:

Mama Bear <u>poured</u> porridge <u>into the bowls</u>.

I use the last page of the book to illustrate an *interpretive* (Think and Search) question. It states that when Goldilocks opened her eyes and saw the bears, she screamed and ran out the door. I ask the question:

How did Goldilocks feel when she saw the bears?

My students usually laugh and say scared, afraid, petrified, etc. I then ask them how they knew, because it didn't tell them on the page. This is a great way to begin to help them see what it means to read between the lines. When teaching this strategy, I tell my students that I'm more concerned about them knowing *what kind of* QAR they are looking at rather than knowing the answer.

When my students come up to me with a question and say, "I don't get it," or "I can't find the answer," my first response is to tell them what kind of question it is. They then need to tell me how they will look for the answer. Students start coming up to me saying, "I know it is a "Think and Search," so the answer is not right there on the lines, but I need help knowing what paragraphs or pages I need to put together." That is very different from, "I don't get it!"

Beginning with a very easy and familiar book ensures that all students are successful and can really start to understand the concepts. I use easy, familiar materials for at least a week or two. I then start to apply this strategy to more detailed books, and finally to grade-appropriate materials: the books they are reading for enjoyment, as well as their science and social studies texts.

Now, when I write questions to go along with reading assignments, I usually limit the amount to three, one of each kind. On the facing page is an example of the questions students were asked to answer while reading *James and the Giant Peach*. Notice that there is one kind of each QAR.

James and the Giant Peach
Pages 28-47

   1. What happened to Aunt Sponge and Aunt Spiker?

   2. How did all the creatures feel when the peach started to roll? Prove it!

   3. Where do you think they will end up? Why?

Another way to use QARs is to have students write their own questions after reading. My students have traveling strategy folders that they can take and use anywhere they are working: at their desk, in the hall, at a table, in the resource room, at home, etc. (Manila file folders work well.) On the inside of the folder is the reproducible found on the following page. I find that if students have this information right at their fingertips, they use it!

Once a month we look at the folders, and those students who need clean copies get new ones. Usually by the end of each month the QAR sheets are full of "chicken scratches," which shows me they are really using these.

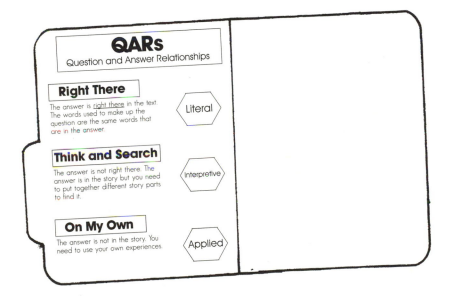

QARs
Question and Answer Relationships

Right There

The answer is <u>right there</u> in the text. The words used to make up the question are the same words that are in the answer.

Literal

Think and Search

The answer is not right there. The answer is in the story but you need to put together different story parts to find it.

Interpretive

On My Own

The answer is not in the story. You need to use your own experiences.

Applied

Responding to Literature

As I moved away from the basal to literature, one concern was "independent work time." What would students be doing in place of workbooks and run-offs? I wanted to encourage more student ownership and participation in responding to the literature.

There was also never the perfect assignment. Some tasks were either too hard for some students or too easy for others. I always had the student who completed the task in five minutes and said, "I'm done; now what do I do?" And in the same classroom, I had students who needed a full day to complete the same assignment and/or were up at my table within five minutes saying, "I don't get it." I had students who were wonderful, creative, and proficient writers. Writing was easy and enjoyable for them. These students had no problems or complaints when it came to answering six to twelve questions per story, or doing three or four pencil/paper tasks.

I also had students who hated to write. It was a difficult task for them; it took all the effort they could muster to answer just two questions. These students were always playing catch-up. Also, with specific questions and worksheets there are usually right and wrong answers. Students rarely expanded their thoughts and responses. We now have a wealth of different ideas and activities students can do as they read. Students choose how they will respond to the piece of literature they are reading.

At first I was concerned about accountability. I wanted to make sure I was addressing the skills and concepts my students needed to know. How was I going to make sure I was adequately addressing comprehension when students were choosing how to respond to their books?

As Regie Routman writes in her book, *Invitations:*

> Initially teachers find it difficult to believe that comprehension is being adequately addressed. As teachers, we have been used to requiring lengthy responses, book reports, summaries, large numbers of vocabulary words to be looked up, and/or answers to many specific questions. However, when teachers and students look at larger issues from literary and personal perspectives, the important details, major happenings, and themes do emerge.

Open-ended Questions

On pages 30 and 31 are questions that can be applied to most pieces of literature. Students can have access to these in a number of different ways:

- They can be charted and hung on the walls or put together with rings on a chart stand.

- Students can have their own copies of these to keep in their desks. I make a copy for each child and they put them together with paper fasteners.

- We make a big book entitled *Open-Ended Questions*.

All of these are working documents that we add to daily and/or weekly as new ideas and questions are generated.

I. *Characters*

Who is the main character? Describe him/her/it.

Do you like the main character? Why or why not?

Who are the minor characters?

Are the minor characters necessary? Why or why not?

Do you know anyone like the characters in the books?

What problems do the characters have?

Who was your favorite character? Why?

What does the main character want?

What have you learned from one of your characters?

Analyze and/or write the story from another point of view.

What characters have gone through changes and growth throughout the story? Describe them.

Write a diary entry as if you were one of the characters.

II. *Setting*

Where does this story take place?

How is the setting important to the story?

Why do you think the story takes place in_____?

How would the story be different if it took place in_____ at _____?

III. *Plot*

What is happening in the story?

How did the story end?

Change the ending.

What was the climax of the story?

What events led to the climax?

Could any events have been left out? Why or why not?

What are the problems?

How are the characters trying to resolve those problems?

Have you ever been in a situation like this?

Add a chapter or new incident.

IV. Theme

What is the theme of the story?

V. Personal Reactions

What is your favorite part of the story? Why?

What was the funniest part? Saddest? Happiest? Scariest?

What would happen if . . .?

What would you have done if you were . . .?

Why do you think the book is titled_____?

What does the author do to make you want to keep reading?

What surprised you the most? Why?

Make some predictions.

What experiences have you had that were similar in the story?

These are only a sampling of open-ended questions that students can respond to. Some of the questions fit into more than one category. One year, my students wanted to categorize the questions into the story elements like we have done here. Another year, my students just wanted to list them, in no specific categories.

It is difficult for many students to take control of their own learning, especially when they come from environments where they have been given the assignments and are told what to do and how to do it. We need to demonstrate and model (see pages 20 and 21) before expecting students to go beyond the very literal responses we often get. My goal is to get students to look critically at the text, examine those underlying connections and meanings, and relate them to their own lives.

Another activity that I often do is to have students generate questions about the story that have no correct answers. This really helps them to think critically and go beyond those one-correct-answer questions, which usually are literal.

Meaningful Literature Extensions

Some of my students need no structure or guidance when responding to their reading. They usually use their language arts notebook and start with a blank piece of paper. Other students can't begin with a blank piece of paper. It is too overwhelming, and they need some structure and guidance. The activities and ideas on pages 32 and 33 are used to help students who need some extra support in coming up with ways to respond to their book.

I have a set of stackable trays in the classroom. As we introduce new ideas, appropriate worksheets get put into a tray and are available for students to use all year. Some of my students actually complete the papers, while others use them as a catalyst for another idea. I have trays containing worksheets for the following ideas:

The following activities do not involve the use of specific papers found in the stackable trays. They are more creative, and some involve the use of art.

Book Jackets

Students can create new book jackets for their stories. They need to do a writing component that tells why they designed a new cover and the significance of what they put on the new book jacket.

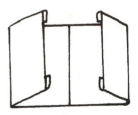

Murals

This activity can be done in pairs or small groups. Students can create a mural about the characters, summarize the story, sequence the story, show their favorite parts, etc. For example, see the mural of *Charlie and the Chocolate Factory* in the picture on page 7.

Dioramas

Dioramas can be made of students' favorite parts, a new ending, a new chapter, describing the character, etc.

Mobiles

Students can make mobiles of specific characters and their traits, vocabulary words, main idea and supporting details, etc.

Storyboards
See page 96.

Other activities may include:

poems
newspaper articles
letters
persuasive paragraphs
journal or diary entries written from the character(s) point of view

Students are responsible for making sure that they do a variety of different activities. The form on the following page is what students use to keep track of the different activities they do each day. Students put the date in each box that corresponds to their response for the day.

For example, one day the child chooses to complete the reproducible on page 50. He will put the date in a box under Characters.

The next day he chooses to use the reproducible on page 55 to compare and contrast two different characters. He will put the date in a box under Characters.

The fifth day the student writes a prediction about what will happen next in the story. He writes the date in a box under personal reactions.

Free Responses

Name: _____

Look at the charts for some ideas! HOW ARE YOU FEELING ABOUT THE BOOK? Put today's date in a box under the heading of your response. When using your *Own Ideas*, make sure you write down specifically what you've done (diorama prediction, poem, news article, etc.)

Characters
3/8 3/9 ☐ ☐ ☐ ☐ ☐ ☐ ☐

Setting
☐ ☐ ☐ ☐ ☐ ☐ ☐ ☐ ☐

Plot
☐ ☐ ☐ ☐ ☐ ☐ ☐ ☐ ☐

Theme and Mood
☐ ☐ ☐ ☐ ☐ ☐ ☐ ☐ ☐

Personal Reactions
3/12 ☐ ☐ ☐ ☐ ☐ ☐ ☐ ☐

Own Ideas
What did you do? Be specific!
☐ 3/10 ☐ ☐ ☐ ☐ ☐ ☐ ☐

Newspaper article

The third day the child begins a newspaper article describing an event that took place in the book. He will write the date under Own Ideas. *He must then, under the box, also write down specifically what he has done.* If the child works on the article on the fourth day, he puts an arrow in the next box.

Free Responses

Name: _____

Look at the charts for some ideas! HOW ARE YOU FEELING ABOUT THE BOOK? Put today's date in a box under the heading of your response. When using your *Own Ideas*, make sure your write down specifically what you've done (diorama, prediction, poem, news article, etc.).

Characters

Setting

Plot

Theme and Mood

Personal Reactions

Own Ideas
What did you do? Be specific!

Vocabulary Development

Vocabulary development for students in grades three through six plays an integral part in their learning throughout all subject areas.

We found ourselves in a vicious cycle when it came to vocabulary development. Students were "learning" vocabulary for the week. They knew how to "play the game." They memorized the key vocabulary for the unit or section we were working on; they did a great job copying the definitions from dictionaries and then spitting back those definitions. Using the word in a sentence of their own was another activity they could get by with. (Many of them used the same basic sentence from the dictionary, but changed one or two words.)

Yet there was no carryover from week to week, never mind month to month. After science and/or social studies units were completed, students quickly forgot any new vocabulary they encountered. The same thing happened with books they were reading.

When students were asked to "add more" or "revise," they often came back up to my desk with the word "really" or "very" added. For example, one student had written the sentence:

"It was bright."

I asked him to go back to his seat and add more to make the sentence come alive. We were reading the book, *James and the Giant Peach*, and I was hoping he might use the word "luminous" rather than bright. (We had just read the section where James gets the gems and describes them as luminous.) When the student came back with his new sentence it read:

"It was very bright!"

The following activities and ideas help students internalize new vocabulary words and relate them to things/concepts they already understand. The goal is to help students take ownership of the words so they truly understand them, and will then use them in their daily writing and discussions.

Vocabulary Books

We usually make a class book for all science and social studies units and books we read. Students each select one vocabulary word they've learned and are interested in. They write the word on a piece of construction paper and then do anything they want to show the meaning of the selected word. Choices include, but are not limited to:

using definitions
using the word in a sentence
drawing pictures
cutting out pictures from magazines and newspapers
using acronyms
using synonyms and antonyms
making webs and charts
comparing and contrasting
list associations
parts of speech
suffixes and prefixes that can be added

One of my classes had read the book, *Call it Courage*, at the beginning of the school year. Midyear they were doing some experiments to understand the concept of density. One activity they did was to try floating an egg in tap water. The egg sank. Then they added salt and the egg came floating to the top. As this happened, one of the students called out, "Hey, that water is brackish!" When asked how he knew that, he stated he had remembered the page in the vocabulary notebook the class had made for *Call it Courage*, where someone had drawn waves and glued salt all over them to illustrate the word *brackish*.

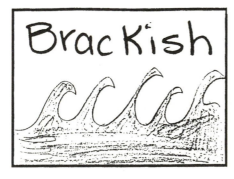

This student covered the waves with glue and sprinkled salt all over it.

This child said, "Number 1, they are enemies. Number 2, they have a truce, and number three, they talk."

Bookmarks

Give students new bookmarks for each book they read. I use oaktag and cut 3" x 9" strips on the paper cutter. As students read, they keep track of words they are unfamiliar with on the bookmarks. The only thing that is written is the word and the page number. (In the past, I tried this activity but had students write what they thought the word meant on the bookmark and then look it up in the dictionary. Needless to say, they *rarely* brought any words to reading groups. It was too much work. By merely noting the word and page number on the bookmarks, students are not overwhelmed by additional work as they read.)

Students are accountable for the bookmarks! After each book is completed, the bookmarks go into their portfolios, whether they have anything written on them or not! At the end of each month, or at the end of each marking period, we take out the bookmarks. Some students have many words on each bookmark, and some have empty bookmarks. Because we keep the bookmarks and review them monthly or quarterly, students are truly accountable for vocabulary, and put more effort into vocabulary development as they read.

sustenance
pg. 20

reverie
pg. 28

sauntered
pg. 32

stockpiles
p.g. 39

Crossword Puzzles

This is a popular activity with students. They can use any size graph paper to make the puzzles. First, students put the words into the squares in a crossword puzzle form.

Next, they take a marker and make a box around each word.

Words are then numbered with a marker.

Students now write the clues.

Across
1. sadness ; sorrow
3. the central part of a church

Down
2. an undersized animal

The last thing they do is to take a piece of thin paper (the copy paper used in copy machines or newsprint works well), place it over the graph paper and trace the boxes and numbers without the words/answers. The boxes and numbers show through the paper very boldly because they were traced with markers.

Word Searches

My students love to make word searches, but I didn't support this activity because they really didn't have to understand the words or do anything with them. All they had to do was write the words on graph paper and then have someone find them.

We have added a new twist so that students are doing something to develop and understand their vocabulary while doing these word searches. The words need to be categorized by the way they are placed in the search (see the example below). Words can be placed in any of these ways:

horizontally:
>   left to right on top half of page
>   left to right on bottom half of page

vertically:
>   top to bottom on left side of page
>   top to bottom on right side of page
>   bottom to top on left side of page
>   bottom to top on right side of page

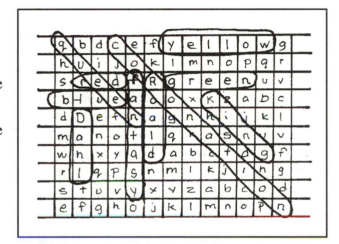

diagonally:
>   left to right (top to bottom)
>   left to right (bottom to top)

Students have to place their words for other students to find based on categories.

In the illustration, for instance:

- color words (red, blue, green, yellow) are placed horizontally, left to right, on the top part of the puzzle.

- words for genres and authors (fantasy, Roald, and Dahl) are placed vertically, from top to bottom, on the left side of the puzzle.

- nobility/dynasty words (coronation, queen, king) are placed from top to bottom, diagonally.

ABC Books

Jerry Pallotta has fantastic alphabet books in the science area for older students. Some titles include:

The Ocean Alphabet Book
The Frog Alphabet Book
The Flower Alphabet Book
The Icky Bug Alphabet Book
The Bird Alphabet Book
The Yucky Reptile Alphabet Book
The Victory Garden Alphabet Book

We usually make an alphabet book for each science and social studies unit. We begin by working in a whole-class group. I lay a set of alphabet cards out on the floor. We also have available a stack of index cards or paper cut into squares. We brainstorm any words or concepts we can think of related to the unit we just studied. We write words on the index cards or pieces of paper and put them under the corresponding letter.

Students may also come up with phrases or sentences. For example, after studying a unit on magnets, one student said, "Opposite poles attract." We write that on a card and it can go under the letter "P" for "poles" or "A" for "attract." Many times, students begin to describe what the word means, but can't think of the exact vocabulary word. At that point someone else usually remembers, or we get out our textbook and try to find it.

After we have brainstormed as many words as we can, we then go to our textbooks and look for boldface words and new concepts. When we have exhausted our lists of words, we then look at the alphabet and see what letters aren't represented. We think about how to represent that letter. Many times we just write a sentence about something we've learned which contains a word beginning with that letter.

Each student then picks a letter and the corresponding word or words to illustrate and write for our ABC book.

Envelopes

We have three shoeboxes in our room.

For each science unit, social studies unit and novel we read, there is a set of cards containing vocabulary words that correspond to the unit or book. On one side of each card is a vocabulary word. In the top right-hand corner of the card is the page number where that word can be found in context. On the back of the card is a definition.

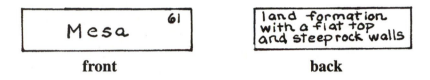

front   **back**

As we complete each unit and/or book, the vocabulary cards go into an envelope and are put into the corresponding shoebox. Now these words are available for students to use and refer back to all year. (You can also have a box for math.)

Once a month we have a vocabulary review. I take the envelopes out and place them around the room. The corresponding science book, social studies book or novel is also put with each envelope. Students work either in pairs or in small groups. Each pair or group of students begins at an envelope. I set a timer. Students have about five or six minutes to take out all of the words from their envelope. They can:

- sort and classify them
- review the definitions
- look at the page where the word is found in context
- use them in sentences.

When the timer goes off, each group goes to the next envelope.

This is an excellent way keep up the students' vocabulary skills. In June, they are still reviewing words they worked with in September and October.

Sorting

Using the envelopes described on page 41, students sort the words, using one of two basic kinds of sorting activities. In closed sorts, I tell the students in advance what the main categories are. With open sorts, I don't give the students any criteria for grouping. They must search for meanings and discover relationships without knowing the main categories.

Categorizing

This requires students to determine relationships among terms much in the same way as open and closed sorts. The difference lies in the structure. For example, students are given four to six words and are asked to do something with them. For example:

- Cross out the word in each set that does not belong.
- On the line above the set, write a word or phrase that explains the relationship among the remaining three words.

_____	_____
tides	plain
waves	continental shelf
seaweed	trench
currents	continental slope

- Circle the word in each group that includes the others.

government	throne
council	crown
judges	coronation
governor	church

One fifth-grade classroom divided itself into four groups. Each group was given the vocabulary words from their science unit to put into categories.

One group of students grouped the words into four categories:

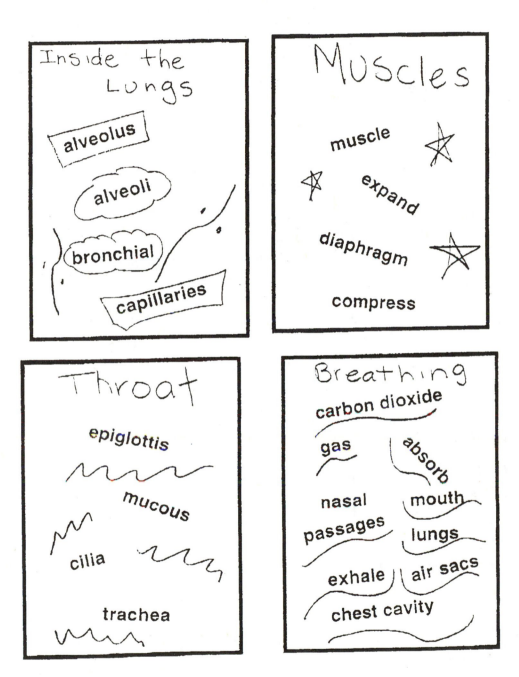

Inside the Lungs

alveolus

alveoli

bronchial

capillaries

Muscles

muscle

expand

diaphragm

compress

Throat

epiglottis

mucous

cilia

trachea

Breathing

carbon dioxide

gas

absorb

nasal passages

mouth

lungs

exhale

air sacs

chest cavity

Another group put the words into six categories.

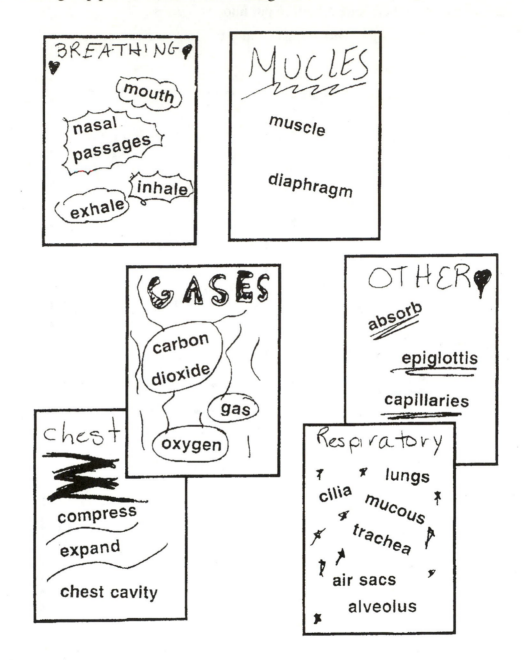

There is no one "right way." However, each group had to justify its categories and the words placed in each.

Analogies

Word analogies relate a familiar concept to an unfamiliar concept. They also trigger critical thinking about relationships.

Some types of analogies

1. Part to whole
   burner : stove : : faucet: _____

2. Person to situation
   Lincoln : slavery : : _____ : Independence

3. Synonym
   elated : joyful : : unhappy: _____

4. Antonyms
   pinch : handful : : gulp: _____

I have students keep track of unfamiliar words they encounter while reading, and write each word down on a Post-it. When we have our reading group, students bring the Post-its and we try to categorize these words. Many times the majority of students bring the same word or words. Sometimes I tell students that they need to bring three Post-its to the next group meeting. They often try to find words that no one will know.

Remember, effective comprehension and vocabulary instruction take place before, during and after reading.

Big Books

The more students can link the new to the known, the greater the understanding of the new. We use class Big Books to help relate words to each other and bridge that unknown with the known. For example, look at the following list of words. Most of our students would understand their meanings.

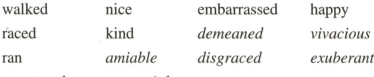

walked	nice	embarrassed	happy
raced	kind		
ran			

By using these familiar vocabulary words, we can now link new vocabulary to the known.

walked	nice	embarrassed	happy
raced	kind	*demeaned*	*vivacious*
ran	*amiable*	*disgraced*	*exuberant*
sauntered	*congenial*		
promenaded			
meandered			

These words can also be "numbered" or put into the order of intensity, from most to least intense or least to most intense. There is really no right or wrong order.

This activity leads to great discussions. Students have to be able to justify why they think one word might be more significant in terms of feelings than another.

I have seen an incredible carryover into students' writing by using these Big Books. Students see how the choice of words gives their writing new meaning. For example:

He was feeling badly.

He was feeling desolate.

There is a different tone to these two sentences, just because of the choice of words used.

All of my students have a pack of Post-its. While reading, when they come to a word that they think fits into one of our Big Books, they write it down and put the Post-it on the page in the Big Book where they think it belongs. At some point during the day or week we go through the Big Books and figure out where all the new words belong.

Some of our Big Book titles include:

Feelings	*Ways of Moving*
Describing Characters	*Setting Words*
Instead of Said	*Weather Words*

Part III
Activities

Character Development

Activities

The Pinballs is a great book to use because of the three main characters.

Brainstorm the meaning of the word *pinballs*. What words do students associate with the word pinball? Write down students' responses on a large piece of paper cut out in the shape of a pinball.

As the book is read, discuss how the three children have the same characteristics that were brainstormed on the paper pinball. Add to the pinball throughout the story.

As students read, they can fill in the form found on the following page. Think about why the characters act the way they do.

The Pinballs
by Betsy Byars

Three very different children come to live together in a foster home. They feel like pinballs because they have no control over where they go or what they do.

Literature Extensions

Students can write about a time in their life when they might have felt like a pinball. If students can't think of one, they can write about another person they know who probably feels or felt like a pinball.

Using Any Book

Students can use the worksheet on the following page to follow one character throughout their whole story. Instead of using each section for a different character, use sections for the beginning, middle and end of the book.

This sheet can also be added to on a daily basis as students continue to read and learn about the characters.

Title _____

Character	Physical Description / Age	Personality: Prove it!	Changes / Growth

Character Development

Activities

There are a number of main and minor characters that can be studied and explored in this book:

> Little Willy
> Searchlight
> Grandfather
> Stone Fox
> Clifford Snyder

As students discuss and describe the characters, we make a list of those descriptive words. We put them into Big Books. See page 45 for more information on making and using vocabulary Big Books.

Students need to give specific sentences and paragraphs from the book that back up their opinion about certain characters.

Stone Fox
by John
Reynolds Gardiner

Little Willy, a ten-year-old boy, enters a race with his dog Searchlight in order to win money to pay the back taxes on his grandfather's farm.

Literature Extensions

Using the reproducible on the following page, have students choose characters from the book *Stone Fox* and explore their traits. For example:

| Character's Name & Trait **Little Willy Determined** | → | Evidence from Story |

He was determined to:

find out what was wrong with grandfather.

take care of his grand-father himself.

harvest the potatoes.

pay back the taxes.

win the race.

 ## Using Any Book

Have students draw a picture of a character from the book they are reading. After the picture is complete they can write descriptive words, either on the character or around him or her.

Students can also use the reproducible on the following page to prove that their character has those traits.

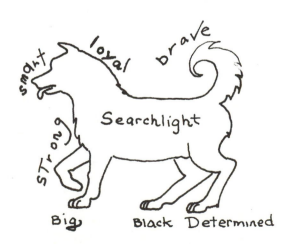

Name _____ Title _____

| Character's Name & Trait | → | Evidence From Story |

| Character's Name & Trait | → | Evidence From Story |

| Character's Name & Trait | → | Evidence From Story |

Compare and Contrast

Activities

Make a chart like the one below.

Night Before Christmas	Cajun Night Before Christmas	Santa Cows

Santa Cows
by Cooper Edens

Cajun Night Before Christmas
Edited by Howard Jacobs

The Night Before Christmas
(any copy)

These are three versions of *The Night Before Christmas.*

This chart can be made on mural paper and hung up in the room so students can all write on it.

Students can compare and contrast:

illustrations   plot
rhythm and rhyme   details

Santa Cows and *Cajun Night Before Christmas* have become some of my students' favorite books to hear over and over again. I find myself reading them at least once a month during the read-aloud time. The rhythm and rhyme are wonderful.

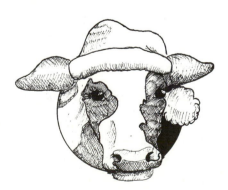

Literature Extensions

Students can work individually or in pairs to make up their own version of *The Night Before Christmas.*

 ## Using Any Book

Students can make a chart like the one shown in the activities section to compare and contrast any of the following:

three characters in a book(s)
three different books by the same author
three different authors' styles

The following three books are different variations of *King Arthur.* Students enjoy comparing these.

King Arthur, by Howard Pyle,
Knights of the Round Table, adapted by
          Gwen Gross
Excalibur, by Carol Heyer

Compare and Contrast

Activities

There are a wealth of *Cam Jansen* books available. All of these books have a number of things that remain the same:

- the genre is "mysteries"
- same characters: Cam, Eric
- Cam uses her photographic mind to help solve the mysteries

Many things in the books are also different:

- characters
- setting
- plot

I usually read one *Cam Jansen* book during a read-aloud time, and then we read another book together as a class. These books, the one read aloud and the one assigned, become the two books used for this activity.

Fill in the reproducible on the following page as a class.

Some other good resources for comparing and contrasting include:

Boxcar Kid Books
American Girls Collection
Bunnicula Books
Encyclopedia Brown Books
Nate the Great Books

 ## Using Any Book

Students can use the Venn diagram to compare and contrast any of the following within a single book or using two or more books:

different books	settings
by the same author	sequels
characters	plots
chapters	

Most of David Adler's *Cam Jansen* books start with the title:

Cam Jansen and the Mystery of the . . .

I did not write down the name of a specific Cam Jansen book because any of them will work well.

Literature Extensions

Have students each pick another *Cam Jansen* book to read and fill in a Venn diagram comparing it to one of the two books used during the activity.

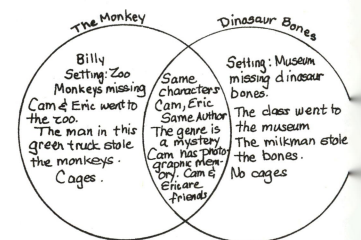

For a challenge, students can also add a third circle to compare three items.

The Venn diagram above was created by a third grader as she compared and contrasted two *Cam Jansen* books.

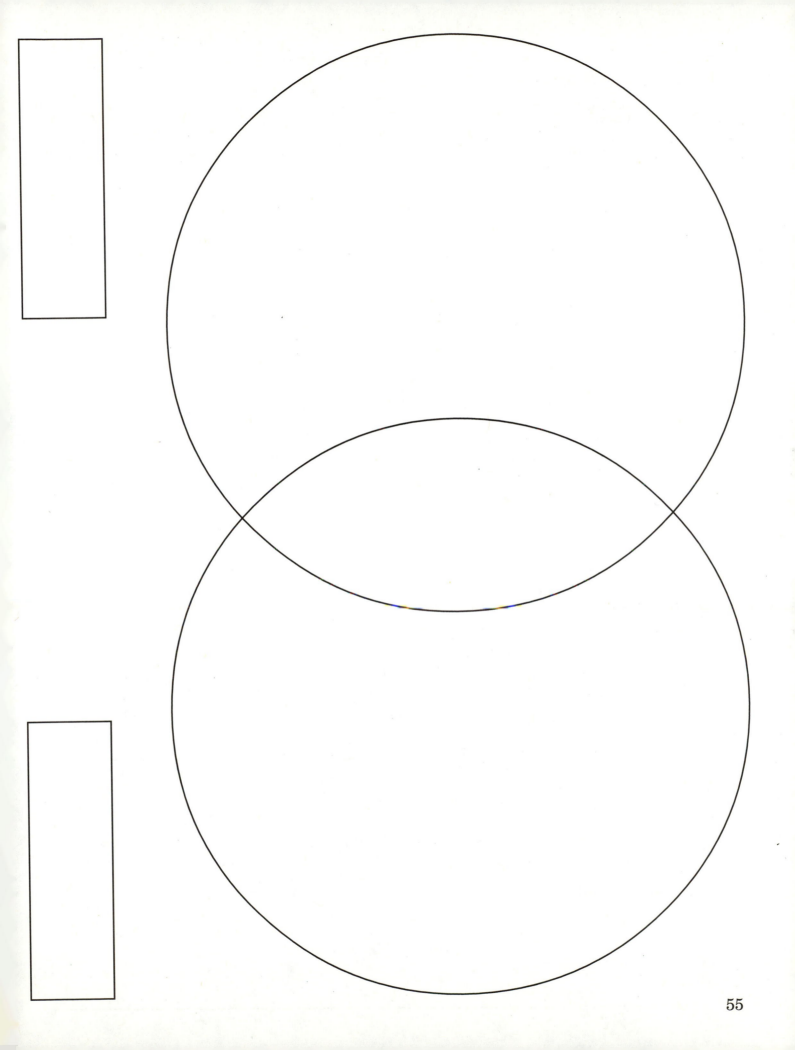

55

Drawing Conclusions

Activities

Cam Jansen mysteries are great books to use when learning about the skill of drawing conclusions.

Cam constantly draws conclusions based on things she sees and remembers. Discuss some of the conclusions she comes up with and what she bases those decisions on. For example, she and her friends noticed that the monkeys were missing. Cam drew a number of conclusions:

The monkeys are fed in their cages.
(There were banana peels in the cages left over from the last feeding.)

The monkeys were not being moved.
(If the monkeys were being moved they would all have been taken.

                and

The guard would have told them if the zoo had moved the monkeys.)

None of the guards stole the monkeys.
(The guards have keys and would not have had to cut the lock.)

Brainstorm times when students have come to a conclusion based on some evidence. Was their conclusion correct? What was the evidence that led them to that decisions?

I usually begin this activity with a story about a missing piece of chocolate cake and a younger brother or sister with chocolate all over the face and clothes. What conclusions can be drawn?

Cam Jansen and the Mystery at the Monkey House
by David Adler

Cam and her friends go to the zoo and discover that the monkeys are missing.

Literature Extensions

Have students choose another *Cam Jansen* mystery. Use the reproducible on the following page to write down conclusions Cam makes and how she gets to those conclusions.

Some other *Cam Jansen* books include:

> *Cam Jansen and the*
> *Mystery of the Stolen Diamonds*
> *Mystery of the Babe Ruth Baseball*
> *Mystery of the Monster Movie*
> *Mystery of the Carnival Prize*

 ## Using Any Book

Use the same reproducible as described above to organize conclusions that characters in different books make.

Encyclopedia Brown books, written by Donald Sobol, are also excellent resources for students to use when working with the skill of drawing conclusions.

Name _____

Date _____

Book Title _____

Based on What Evidence

Conclusions

Drawing Conclusions

Activities

Casey and her friends draw many conclusions about this new neighbor. Brainstorm some of these conclusions and how the children make them. What are they basing these conclusions on? How much is their imagination affecting these conclusions?

For example:

The animals could be part dog and might have escaped from the zoo.

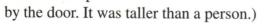

(The animals were big and hairy. They had the longest legs Cat had ever seen. Their tails hung down like elephant trunks. One reared up by the door. It was taller than a person.)

The neighbor is a monster, werewolf, spy or bank robber. He probably has money buried in the cellar and is hunted by the police.

(The man was wearing a bandanna over his face. He is not friendly. Something big and lumpy, wrapped in a blanket, was unpacked.)

At one point in the story Benny yells that the food they were given is poisoned. Why does he come up with this conclusion? What is it based on?

Mystery on October Road by Alison Cragin Herzig and Jane Lawrence Mali

A mysterious man and his two huge animals have moved next door to Casey. She and her friends are determined to find out all about him.

Literature Extensions

How would the conclusions that Casey and her friends make change if things were different in the book? For example:

What if the neighbor didn't wear a bandanna over his face?
What if the neighbor were a woman?
What if the neighbor waved to the children?

Have students choose a conclusion that was made by Casey and her friends. They can write what things led to that conclusion.

Students can then revise what happened in the book so that Casey and her friends come up with a different conclusion.

Have students share their revisions and then ask peers what the new conclusion might be.

Using Any Book

Have students think about conclusions their characters are making. What actions and/or events led to those conclusions? What would happen if the actions and/or events were different?

Figurative Language

Activities

Writers INC defines figurative language as "a language which cannot be taken literally since it was written to create a special effect or feeling."

As students are reading have them look for figurative language:

> "Oh, go fly a kite."
> "You're supposed to rise."
> "Pot the window box plants."
> "Patch the front screen door."

Some of the sayings and/or sentences that are found in the book are not necessarily figurative language, but words that can have different meanings. Talk about the differences between the two. Talk about the problems when both are taken literally, whether it's the use of the wrong meaning or figurative language.

Students can fill in the reproducible on the following page.

Some other titles are:

> *Amelia Bedelia and the Baby*
> *Amelia Bedelia Goes Camping*
> *Amelia Bedelia Helps Out*
> *Amelia Bedelia and the Surprise Shower*
> *Come Back Amelia Bedelia*

Good Work, Amelia Bedelia
by Peggy Parish

Although the activities on this page have been done with a specific book, any *Amelia Bedelia* book would be appropriate to use.

Literature Extensions

Make a figurative language book. Each student can write down a sentence that deals with figurative language, and illustrate each page exactly as the sentence reads, so that it becomes a nonsense book. All of the pages can be bound together to make a class book.

 ## Using Any Book

Have students look for examples of figurative language in their book.

As students think about the book they are each reading, have them come up with some things that might be said among their characters. For example, would any of their characters say to each other, "Oh, go fly a kite!"? Why or why not?

Would this enhance their book? Why or why not?

Figurative Language

What it really means

Figurative Language

What it really means

Figurative Language

What it really means

Figurative Language

What it really means

Figurative Language

Activities

Students can use the reproducible on the previous page to fill in as they are reading.

Here are some statements found in the book:

"Is all this really true . . . or are you pulling my leg?"

"Charlie, you mark my words."

"All right Mother, keep your hair on!"

"He'll need it, the skinny little shrimp."

"Just look at him! He's laughing his head off."

"Control yourself! Pull yourself together!"

"He's bound to come out in the wash."

"Old Fickelgruber would give his front teeth . . ."

"My goodness, she is a bad nut after all . . ."

"Are you off your rocker?"

Fred Gwyne has some great books that play with language. They are:

The King Who Rained
A Little Pigeon Toad
The Sixteen-Hand Horse
A Chocolate Moose for Dinner

Using Any Book

Using the reproducible on the following page, students can choose a saying that one of their characters might say to another. For example, which of their characters would give their front teeth for _____?

Have them use their characters' names in the statement section.

James and the Giant Peach
by Roald Dahl

This is a story about an orphaned boy named James who discovers a huge peach growing in the back yard. Inside the peach live a group of incredible characters. They have many exciting adventures together before landing in New York City.

Literature Extensions

Make a class book titled: *What I really meant was . . .*

Have students each choose a sentence that has figurative language in it. Use the reproducible on the following page as a format for the book. The pictures the students create are hysterical!

"Just look at him!
He's laughing his head off."

Title _____

Statement

No!!

What I really meant was

Flashbacks

Activities

Flashbacks occur in stories when the author returns to an earlier time in a story in order to help the reader understand what is happening and why it might be happening.

Brainstorm what flashbacks are and how they are used. Use the reproducible on the following page to organize and understand the flashbacks in this story.

Avalanche
by Arthur Roth

Chris Palmer is a boy who goes out to hunt and ski for the day. He sets off an avalanche by shooting his rifle at a coyote. He becomes buried alive under a mountain of snow.

Literature Extensions

Students can use the reproducible on the following page to help them understand the flashbacks in *Avalanche*. Have them fill out the sections as they read. It might take students three days to complete the activity. After reading each chapter, they can fill in one section of the reproducible.

 ## Using Any Book

Have students write a flashback to go along with the book they are reading. They can flash back to an earlier time in their character's life.

What is happening?

Is the character happy? Why?

Describe an incident that might have happened in the character's past to make him/her behave or feel the way he/she does today in the book.

Try using flashbacks when writing autobiographies.

1. What is happening in the story before the
flashback occurs? Pages _____ Give a summary.

2. The Flashback Page _____

Where does the flashback take you?
Why is it important to know this information?
Why has the flashback occurred at this point in the story?

3. Where does the story return after the flashback?
Pages _____

How does the flashback help you understand what is happening in the story?
Why has the story returned to this specific time? place? part?

Inferencing

Activities

This book has no chapter titles. As each chapter is read and discussed, talk about the plot and the theme.

Sometimes chapter titles are directly related to a specific incident in the chapter. Such titles are very literal.

Other times chapter titles have nothing to do with a specific action or incident in the story, but are based on inferences that can be made about the chapter.

Have students brainstorm some literal and inferential titles for the same chapter. Talk about the differences.

Island of the Blue Dolphins
by Scott O'Dell

This is a survival story about Karana, an Indian girl who lives alone for years on the Island of the Blue Dolphins.

Literature Extensions

Using the reproducible on the following page, have students decide upon some chapter titles. They can make up two titles for each chapter, one literal and the other inferential.

Some other good books that have no chapter titles are:

Pinballs, by Betsy Byars
Skinnybones, by Barbara Park
Almost Staring Skinnybones, by Barbara Park
Avalanche, by Arthur Roth

Most of Gary Paulsen's books have no chapter titles.

 ## Using Any Book

Students can use the reproducible on the following page with any book they are reading, regardless of whether or not the books have chapter titles. If their book does not have chapter titles, then the sheet can be filled in as explained above in *Literature Extensions*.

If their book does have chapter titles, then the reproducible can be used differently. Have students write down the chapter titles and then think about the following questions. They can also write down some of their feelings.

Why did the author create that title?
Do they agree or disagree about the chapter title?
Is the chapter title based on an incident or an inference?
Give the chapter a new title. Defend the new title.

Creating Chapter Titles

Name: _____

Title: _____

Author: _____

Pages:_____   Chapter Title _____

Why?

Pages: _____   Chapter Title _____

Why?

Pages: _____   Chapter Title _____

Why?

Main Idea/ Supporting Details

Activities

Talk about the differences between a main idea and the supporting details. Use the reproducible found on the following page and fill it in, using the book *Stellaluna.* For example:

Main Idea:

Stellaluna got lost.

Supporting Details:

An owl attacked Stellaluna and her mom.
Stellaluna's tiny wings would not allow her to fly.
She fell onto a branch.
Hours later she let go of the branch and fell into a bird's nest.

Main Idea:

Stellaluna learned to be like the birds.

Supporting Details:

She stayed awake all day.
She slept during the night.
She didn't hang by her feet.
She learned to land gracefully on a branch.

Stellaluna
by Janell Cannon

Stellaluna is a baby bat who gets lost from its mother and ends up with a family of birds.

Literature Extensions

What would happen if the main idea of the story changed?

What if Stellaluna landed:

in a child's hand?
in the ocean?
in another kind of animal's home?

How does changing the main idea change all of the supporting details? Which details could stay the same? Which ones would have to change?

Using Any Book

Students can use the reproducible on the following page and apply it to any book they are reading.

Name _____

Book Title _____

Date _____

Main Idea

Supporting Details

Metaphors

Activities

Discuss what metaphors are: the comparing of two things in which the words "like" or "as" are not used. Point out the difference between metaphors and similes.

The book *Hailstones and Halibut Bones* is full of metaphors.

> "Time is purple."
> "Gold is the sunshine"
> "Brown is the color of work
>   And the sound of a river"
> "White is a pair of whispers
>   talking."

Using Any Book

Have students pick out some important characters, objects, concepts, etc., from their books and write some metaphors to describe them.

Hailstones and Halibut Bones
by Mary O'Neill

This book is full of poems about colors.

Literature Extensions

Have students each choose a color and write some poems about them that include metaphors. Try using colors other than the basics, such as:

Magenta
Plum
Ivory
Teal
Fuschia
Royal
Chartreuse

Students can also create watercolor pictures to go along with their poems.

Parts of Speech/ Adjectives

Activities

I find it easier for students to understand adjectives when I teach adjectives in conjunction with nouns. We talk about adjectives being the words that make nouns "come alive." They give us a clearer, more detailed picture of a person, place or thing.

Give students a piece of paper. Have them fold it in half. Write a noun on the board, and ask students to draw a picture of it on the left side of their paper. For example, write the word "apple" on the board. Students' pictures of the apple are all different: different colors, shapes, sizes, textures, etc. Then write the following on the board: "the small, green, rotten apple". Now have students draw a picture of this apple on the right side of their paper. The pictures are now more alike because of the adjectives.

After reading the story, have students work together or in groups to find pairs or groups of adjectives and nouns. For example:

slow-flying geese
small, white farmhouse
old broom
cold, autumn night
moonlit sky
tired broom
lonely widow

The Widow's Broom
by Chris Van Allsburg

Minna, a lonely widow, finds a witch's broom and takes it home. The broom comes to life and begins helping Minna around the house. However, the neighbors aren't as happy about the broom as Minna.

Literature Extensions

Students can fill in the diamond on the following page using the directions on page 72. For example:

Mystery

third   person

house   road   woods

dark   eerie   moonlit   desolate

Minna   Mr. Spivey   broom   witch   boys

tired   old   harmless   helpful

lonely   kind   brave

shocked   confused

surprised

Using Any Book

Usually two or three times a month, I ask students to fill in the noun and adjective reproducible (explained above), using the book they are reading. See the two examples on page 73.

Name: _____

Diamond: _____

Title: _____

Author: _____

                                  _____

    _____   _____

_____   _____   _____

_____   _____   _____   _____

_____   _____   _____   _____   _____

_____   _____   _____   _____

_____   _____   _____

    _____   _____

                                    _____

Story Diamond
Nouns and Adjectives

Line 1   Identify the genre

Line 2   Point of view

Line 3   Three nouns explaining the setting
          (Circle one of the nouns)

Line 4   Four adjectives describing the noun you circled

Line 5   Five important nouns in the story
              (2 proper, 3 common)
              Circle a common noun
              Circle a proper noun

Line 6   Four adjectives describing the common noun you circled

Line 7   Three adjectives describing the proper noun you circled

Line 8   Two words describing how you feel about the book

Line 9   One-word summary

This student used the book
Island of the Blue Dolphins
by Scott O'Dell

This Student used the book
James and the Giant Peach
by Roald Dahl

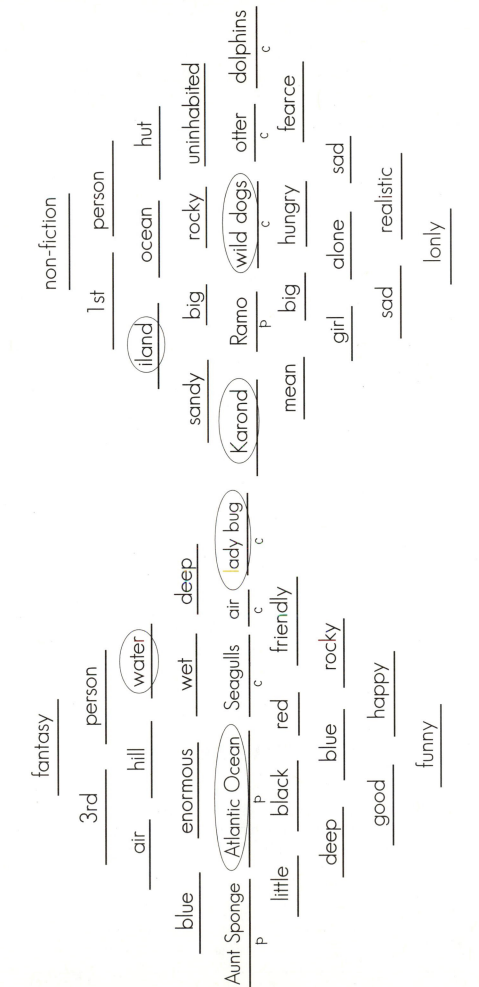

Parts of Speech/Adverbs

Up, Up, and Away
by Ruth Heller

This is a book about adverbs.

Activities

After reading this book, write the categories of adverbs that the book talks about on the board:

Adverbs tell

How?
decently, gently, magically, dreamily, regally

How often?
frequently

When?
recently, today, soon

Where?
there, away

As you read the book, fill in the categories with adverbs the book tells about.

The chart lists the four categories we used; the book does get more detailed. Tailor the categories to the needs of your students and your curriculum.

Literature Extensions

Students can work individually, in small groups, or in pairs to create a class book that can be used to help them all year when they revise their writing.

First they need to brainstorm all the adverbs in each category they can think of. If students are stuck and can't think of any, have them look at books. As soon as they start looking at books their lists grow quickly.

Instead of putting these into a book, words can be put onto index cards and kept in coffee cans or any kind of container.

Using Any Book

I have students fill in the reproducible on the next page at least once a month, using any book they are reading.

So if we have worked with adverbs in November, my students are reviewing the concept from December through June.

Name _____

Date _____

Book Title _____

Find pairs or groups of adverbs and verbs from your book. Categorize them into the following categories:

Adverbs of time	Adverbs of place	Adverbs of manner	Adverbs of degree
When? How often? How long?	Where? To where? From where?	How? (often end in ly)	How much? How little?

Parts of Speech/Nouns

Activities

After reading this book make the following chart on a large piece of mural paper:

Merry-Go-Round and A Cache of Jewels
by Ruth Heller

These books are about nouns.

Common Nouns

damsel   forest   dragon

Proper Nouns

Camelot

Abstract Nouns

hope   love   chivalry
courage   devotion   justice
truth   courtesy

Collective Nouns

tumble of feathers
clamor of birds
bevy of beauties
bouquet of flowers

We used these four major categories of nouns. The book gets more detailed, talking about concrete nouns. We categorized concrete nouns as common nouns.

Literature Extensions

Students can either work individually or together. They will need to choose a book to use. I recommend that they use the one they are reading. Older students will need to choose one page in their book, younger students might need to choose a couple of pages depending on the amount of text on each page.

Using the form on the following page, students can categorize all the nouns they find on their chosen pages. I encourage students to keep a list of ones they are not sure of so we can review those together as a class.

Using Any Book

At least once a month during independent worktime, I ask students to use the reproducible on the following page.

This way, if we have worked on the concept of nouns in October, in June my students are still doing an activity to reinforce and review that skill!

Title of book _____ Pages _____

Common Nouns

Proper Nouns

Abstract Nouns

Collective Nouns

Parts of Speech/Verbs

Activities

After reading this book, make the categories of verbs that the book talks about on the board:

something's being done	action
bloom	fly
run	sail

less action verbs

linking verbs, helping verbs, auxiliary verbs

is	am	are	were	was	am
been	have	has	shall	will	

Fill in the chart with the verbs from the book. Then, using the overhead projector, display a page from a familiar story that students heard when they were younger, such as *Goldilocks* or *Caps For Sale*. Go over each sentence, decide what the verbs are, and add them to the chart. I usually begin with a very easy children's story and then use grade-appropriate materials.

This book discusses many other categories of verbs. Depending upon your students and your curriculum, you may get more detailed than the chart above.

We transfer this information onto a poster or mural. This becomes a skill chart that students can refer back to all year!

Kites Sail High
by Ruth Heller

This is a book about verbs.

Literature Extensions

Students can work in small groups or in pairs to create a class book that can be used to help them all year when they revise their writing.

Have students work individually or in pairs. First they need to brainstorm all the action verbs they can think of, and then categorize the verbs according to topic. Some categories my students came up with are:

> ways to move
> verbs related to people
> happy, sad, mad, etc., verbs

This also ties in well with the Big Book activities explained on page 45.

Using Any Book

Have students choose some sentences from the book they are reading and categorize the verbs. Where would they belong on the chart?

Parts of Speech/Verbs

Activities

Read *The Great Gray Owl* once to enjoy it. As you read it the second time, concentrate on the verbs. This book is very predictable and patterned. Each page begins with a verb that tells something the owl does. For example, the first page says:

"WAKE
Mighty owl
For the sun has set
Proud nocturnal creature
You are no man's pet."

Brainstorm other verbs that pertain to owls.

Have students choose another animal. Using large mural paper, cut out an outline of the animal they choose. Brainstorm all of the verbs that can be associated with the animal. Write them on the mural paper.

Using Any Book

Using the same predictable and repetitive pattern of *The Great Gray Owl,* students can choose a character or animal from the book they are reading and create their own books — for example, using the dog named "Searchlight" from *Stone Fox,* by John Reynolds Gardiner:

RUN
strong friend
your legs carry our future
your strength, our home.

The Great Gray Owl
by Orin Cochrane

The Great Gray Owl is a Big Book that describes an owl. Each page has a verb at the top, and then four sentences giving more detail about the verb.

Literature Extensions

Have students each choose another animal, character or object. Using large construction paper, they can cut out an outline of whatever they choose and then write all the verbs they can think of that pertain to it.

Create a class book titled:

No, I Didn't Walk, I . . .

Students can write the sentence on the top of their paper, filling in the blank and illustrating their sentence. Some ideas my students came up with are:

strolled	sauntered	ran
raced	crawled	danced

We also play a game of charades using these verbs to help students understand the need to expand their use of vocabulary when revising pieces of writing. Students act out:

I walked home.

Then we act out their suggestions:

I strolled home.
I raced home.

We talk about the different picture you get when using words instead of "walk." Students can use this class book to help them revise their writing.

Plurals

Activities

You can either rewrite these poems on chart paper or put them on the overhead so all students can see them.

After reading these poems, make a chart like the one below and categorize the words that are plural. (See pages 18-19 for more information about skill charts.)

word stays the same		
add <u>s</u> to the word		
heads	nails	bags
bricks	bells	horns

add <u>es</u> to the word

change the <u>y</u> to <u>i</u> and add <u>es</u>
french fries

change the <u>f</u> to <u>v</u> and add <u>es</u>
knives

whole word changes	
leaves	people

Ruth Heller's book, *Merry-Go-Round,* and *There's An Ant in Anthony,* by Bernard Most, are also excellent resources to use.

Where the Sidewalk Ends
by Shel Silverstein

"Hector the Collector," pages 46-47

"Sarah Cynthia Sylvia Stout
Would Not Take The Garbage Out," pages 70-71

Both of these poems are full of plural nouns.

Literature Extensions

There's An Ant in Anthony is a book that has many singular nouns. After students read the book they can make their own charts, using legal-sized paper, like the one in the activity. Have them find all of the nouns and categorize them into the appropriate columns based on how the plural would be made.

 ## Using Any Book

Usually once a month I ask students to choose a couple of pages from the book they are reading, find all the nouns, and do the literature extension explained above.

Point of View

Activities

Have students discuss the fact that people have different ideas and impressions (points of view) about a topic or situation.

Talk about the different points of views that certain people will have when involved in the same situation. For example:

> in a busy restaurant —
>> a waitress
>> the owner
>> customers

The waitress may feel overwhelmed and tired, and wish it wasn't so busy. She might even think that a table of customers is being rude and impatient.

However, the table of customers might feel that the waitress is slow and not efficient. They might even wish the restaurant wasn't so busy.

Have students brainstorm a time when they might have been in a situation and seen it from one point of view, while another participant saw it completely differently.

Books written by Bill Peet are excellent resources to use, because most of them are written from the third person point of view, yet they can easily be changed to the character's point of view (first person).

Using Any Book

Students can think about the characters in the book they are reading. How would the story be different if it were written from another point of view?

Most books written by Bill Peet are great resources to use with discussing point of view. Some titles include:

Jennifer and Josephine
Pamela Camel
The Caboose Who Got Loose
How Droofus the Dragon
* Lost His Head*

Cowardly Clyde
Big Bad Bruce
Ella

Literature Extensions

Have students choose a Bill Peet book and rewrite it from one of the characters' point of view, (third person to first person). Using the book *Jennifer and Josephine,* for example, each character can tell the story from this or her own point of view:

Jennifer: "I am not happy about this new owner. He drives me too fast . . ."

Josephine: "I am petrified. This new owner is making my heart beat a mile a minute. I wish we were back at the junkyard . . ."

Mr. Frenzy: "O.K., let's see what
(new owner) this car can do . . ."

Point of View

Activities

Both of these books are written from a first-person point of view.

When using *Dear Mr. Henshaw,* we have a group of three students take on different points of view:

> Leigh Botts
> Mr. Henshaw
> Leigh's mother

How would each student retell the story from his or her character's point of view?

The same activity can be used with *Pedro's Journal.* The characters used are:

> Pedro
> the Captain
> one of the crewmen
> Pedro's mother

Dear Mr. Henshaw
by Beverly Cleary

This book is a collection of letters that a boy named Leigh Botts writes to an author.

Pedro's Journal
by Pam Conrad

This book is told through the eyes of Pedro de Salcedo, a ship's boy aboard Christopher Columbus' ship the *Santa Maria.*

Literature Extensions

Using the reproducible on the next page, students can look at an incident in detail as it was explained in the book, and then look at that incident from another point of view.

I do not want my students putting their energies into copying the text from the book, so I ask them in the first column to give the page numbers and paragraphs (if appropriate), and then a quick summary.

Using Any Book

Have students choose a character from the book they are reading. Write a journal entry from that character's point of view. How would that character describe and feel about something that happened in the book? Would it be different from the way it is described in the book? How? Why?

Students could also write a letter from that character's point of view. The letter could be written to another character in the book. Using the book *James and the Giant Peach,* for example, James could write a letter to Aunt Sponge and Aunt Spiker telling them how he feels about the way he is being treated. Or James could write a letter to the man with the gems, telling him about what has happened since he dropped those gems.

Name _____ Date _____

Book Title _____ Author _____

Incident as written / told in the book	Rewritten from _____ 's point of view	Rewritten from _____ 's point of view
Page(s) _____ Paragraph(s) _____ Summary:		

Predicting

Activities

This is a fast-moving, suspenseful story. It is great to use for predicting, because students can't wait to see what happens next.

As students predict, they need to give reasons why they have predicted a certain outcome. They need to back up their thoughts with evidence from the story, if possible. Some places to stop and ask for predictions are:

page 21, paragraph 1
". . . and a man cooking beside it."

Who is this man?
What will happen next?

page 45

How will Aaron get away?
What plan could he come up with
  to escape?

page 59, paragraph 3

Will this plan work?
Why or why not?

page 71

What is Aaron's idea?

page 78

What will Aaron do?

page 83, paragraph 4
". . . a figure approached . . ."

Who is the figure?

The Half-A-Moon Inn
by Paul Fleischman

Aaron is a twelve-year-old boy who is mute. He is left alone for the first time while his mother goes to town. When a terrible blizzard comes, Aaron sets out to find his mother. But he end up at the mysterious Half-A-Moon Inn, where he meets Miss Grackle.

Literature Extensions

When students have completed their reading assignment, have them fill in the reproducible on the following page.

Using Any Book

Have students make some predictions about the story they are reading:

What will happen next?
Will the problem get solved? How?
Make a prediction about the ending of
  your book.
How will the character get out of the
  situation he/she is in now?

Jim and the Beanstalk, by Raymond Briggs, is another book to use for predicting. Predict what will happen when the giant says:

. . . he doesn't have any teeth.
. . . he used to be a "good-looking lad."

The Frog Prince Continued, by Steve Scieszka, and *Mystery on October Road,* by Alison Cragin Herzig and Jane Lawrence Mali, are also good books to use.

Name _____

Date _____

Book Title _____

My prediction	What really happened

Predicting

Activities

Brainstorm what happens when you make a prediction. Think about the following questions:

> Why did you make the prediction?
> What did you base the prediction on?
> Was the prediction influenced by your past experiences?
> Was it influenced by something that happened in the book?

Have students make many predictions while reading *Fantastic Mr. Fox*. Some great places to stop and predict are:

> page 21:
>
> > What will happen to Mr. Fox? Will the farmers' plan work?
>
> page 36:
>
> > Based on the title, predict what this chapter will be about.
>
> page 53:
>
> > Why did he "let out a shriek of excitement"?

Discuss what it means to back up predictions by evidence in the book or by past personal experiences.

Using Any Book

Usually once a week, or once every other week, I ask students to make a prediction about what is going to happen in their story when they read tomorrow. We have a chart with questions to think about (see activities) for students to refer to.

Fantastic Mr. Fox
by Roald Dahl

Mr. Fox has been stealing the farmyard fowl from three farmers for years. These three mean farmers try to outsmart Mr. Fox.

Literature Extensions

Have students fill out the reproducible on the following page at certain points in the book.

Name _____

Date _____

Book Title _____

My prediction

Back up your prediction.

What evidence did you
use to make this prediction?

Punctuation/ Commas

Activities

This book has commas modeled throughout each chapter. Make a mural like the one shown below and have students write in sentences under the appropriate categories. There are many more rules for the uses of commas than are shown below. Choose the ones that are appropriate for your students and grade level.

Commas Can Be Used
before these conjunctions: but, or, nor, for, yet, and, so
to separate an interjection from the rest of the sentence.
to separate two or more adjectives describing a noun.
to set off dialogue.

The following sentences are only a sampling of the uses of commas found on pages 26-27 of *Bunnicula.*

"I'm not sure yet, but I know there's something funny about that rabbit."

A rabbit, I concluded, is cute to look at, but is generally useless, especially as a companion to dogs.

"Well, what are you talking about?"

No one to play with poor, neglected Harold.

"So?" I asked again, following him, "what have you seen?"

Bunnicula
by James Howe

This mystery-comedy is about three animals: Harold, a dog; Chester, a cat; and Bunnicula, a new pet that comes to live at the house. Chester and Harold are sure that Bunnicula is a vampire bunny.

After a moment, he opened one eye.

So, I would retire each day with my favorite shoe to the rug and chew.

Literature Extensions

After students have read their assigned reading for *Bunnicula,* they can go back and find the sentences that contain commas. Make sure that students are reading for enjoyment and comprehension first, before going back to pick out specific skills.

Have them write the sentences on the mural in the appropriate categories.

Using Any Book

Have students make a chart like the one used in the activity on the left. I usually have them use legal-sized paper. It's a little bigger, and easier for them to make the many categories needed.

Have them search through the book they are reading to find examples of the different uses of commas. Then write each sentence under the appropriate category.

Punctuation/ Commas

No Such Things
by Bill Peet

Bill Peet has created 15 strange and imaginative creatures in this book. He describes each animal.

Activities

This book is written in rhyme, and many of the sentences can be tongue twisters. Pick a sentence that models the use of commas. For example:

> Then they go for a spin, a wild
>   whirling ride,
> Far out in the hilly, broad countryside.

Brainstorm with students on how and why the commas are used. Use the chart explained on page 88 to help them explain and understand the appropriate rules.

Next, have students read the sentence, omitting the commas. How does it sound? Does it make sense?

Have them place commas incorrectly in the sentences. Now what happens? How does the sentence flow? Does it make sense? For example:

> Then they go for a, spin a wild whirling
>   ride
> Far, out in the hilly broad, countryside.

When students have to read the sentences with the inappropriately placed commas, they really get a feel for how and why this convention is used.

Literature Extensions

Have students create their own imaginative animal and write about it. They really enjoy this! Students need to include at least three sentences that use commas for different reasons. (Have them refer back to the chart on page 88 for some help.)

 ## Using Any Book

Have students find a number of sentences from the book they are reading that contain commas. Have them analyze how and why the commas are used.

Students can write down each sentence and explain how the commas help them.

Punctuation/ Quotation Marks

Activities

The littlest cricket has conversations with many animals in this book:

> his mother
> glowworm
> ladybug
> dragonfly
> frog
> the Old One, a spider

Brainstorm all the rules that go along with using quotation marks. Write them on chart paper. (See pages 18-19 for suggestions about using skill charts.)

As students talk about a rule, find where that specific one has been modeled a number of times.

Write some dialogue together. What else might the different characters say to the littlest cricket? Students can work in groups. Each group would take a character and write five things he or she might say to the cricket. What would the cricket say back?

 Using Any Book

Students can write a conversation between a character in their book and a character from another book.

For example, what would their character say to Aunt Sponge and Aunt Spiker? What would Sponge and Spiker say to their character? (Sponge and Spiker are characters from Roald Dahl's book, *James and the Giant Peach.*)

How would their character respond to Bruce, a character in Bill Peet's book, *Big Bad Bruce*?

I Wish I Were a Butterfly
by James Howe

This is a story about a cricket who thinks he is ugly because a frog told him. So he wishes he were a butterfly. The cricket meets and talks with many other animals and starts to believe in himself.

Literature Extensions

Have students write some other adventures and confrontations the cricket might have.

What other animals could the cricket meet? What conversations would they have? How could other animals help support the cricket and help him to feel good about himself? Students need to include dialogue.

Punctuation/ Quotation Marks

The Sign of the Beaver
by Elizabeth George Speare

Twelve-year-old Matt must survive on his own in the Maine wilderness until his father returns. He meets an Indian chief and his grandson, Attean. As Attean and Matt begin to become friends, they teach each other about their lives and customs.

Activities

This book is full of dialogue between Attean and Matt. After reading, take one page and analyze the conventions that go along with the dialogue:

> quotation marks
> indentations
> commas
> periods
> question marks

Discuss the placement of all the conventions.

Have students brainstorm a list of words to use other than the word "said." Put them into a class Big Book for students to use when they are revising their pieces of writing. They can categorize the words into moods/feelings. For example, words that are: happy, sad, positive, negative, etc.

Literature Extensions

Have students write some new dialogue between Attean and Matt.

They could add a new incident, change one of the incidents in the book, change the ending, etc.

Using Any Book

Students can do any of the following activities, depending on the book they are reading. If their book has no dialogue between characters, so there are no quotation marks to find, students can write some conversations between the characters. If their characters did have conversations in the story, what would they say?

If the book they are reading has dialogue, then they can find the quotation marks and other conventions.

As a class activity, have students generate a list of questions they could ask the main character in any book. If they were conducting an interview, what questions would they ask? Students can then write down the responses their characters might give.

Similes

Activities

Talk about similes. Discuss how the use of similes helps create a bold, visual image.

Write the following sentences on sentence strips. Compare the different connotations each sentence has, based on using or not using similes.

> Sam ran down the mountain.
> Sam ran down the mountain like a rabbit.
> Sam ran down the mountain like a turtle.

Below are some similes from the book:

> Inside, Sam felt as cozy as a turtle in its shell.
> The water in the pool was like glass.
> Frightful was as alert as a high tension wire.
> The moon was as big as a pumpkin behind the trees.
> The stars were shining like electric bulbs.
> The icy tree branches shattered like a shopful of crystal.
> The sky was as thick as Indiana bean soup.

My Side of the Mountain
by Jean Craighead George

Sam Gribley is a young man who is tired of living in New York City, so he runs away to the Catskill Mountains. He has no equipment, so he learns to survive with the resources of the wilderness.

Literature Extensions

Have students write a new episode that happened to Sam. Include at least four similes.

Put an object on a desk in the front of the room. Have students describe it using similes. Some great objects to use are marbles, stuffed animals, scenery pictures, and kitchen utensils.

My students started bringing in things from home. We ended up having an object of the week. Each student was responsible for bringing in an object for a specific week.

Using Any Book

At least once a month during independent worktime, I assign similes to students. Using the book they are reading, students need to pick a character or an object in the book, and describe it using similes.

Summarizing

James and the Giant Peach
by Roald Dahl

This is a story about an orphaned boy named James, who discovers a huge peach growing in the back yard. Inside the peach live a group of incredible characters. They have many exciting adventures together before landing in New York City.

Activities

James and the Giant Peach is a great book for summarizing, because it has very distinct episodes that happen.

First, brainstorm with students all the important events in the story. Write down responses on the board.

After students have finished brainstorming, analyze what is on the board. Combine events together, get rid of minor details, order the events, etc. (The first couple of times I do this activity, students have a lot of minor details.)

For example, when discussing the beginning of the book, students brainstormed these following events and I wrote them on the board. We then did revisions:

> James' parents got killed by a
>   rhinoceros.
> James went to live with Aunt Sponge
>   and Aunt Spiker.
> The aunts were mean and nasty.
> They always made James work.
> The aunts were ugly.

became:

> James' parents got killed by a rhinoceros, and so he went to live with two mean, nasty, ugly aunts.

Another example:

> The man gave James some crystals.
> The old man told James to plant the
>   green things and then wonderful
>   thing would happen to him.

became:

> James met an old man who gave him
>   some magic crystals.

Literature Extensions

After the responses from the activity have been analyzed and revised, students can work together in groups and illustrate each episode.

Using Any Book

When students have completed a book, have them do the same activity that was explained above. I want to see all the steps they go through, from brainstorming all the events to combining them to make a summary.

I usually ask students to do this once a month.

Summarizing

Activities

One way of helping students summarize is to fold construction paper into boxes for them to illustrate and/or write in. I usually begin by having students use large construction paper and eventually use the reproducible on page 96.

Big Bad Bruce
by Bill Peet

Bruce is a bear who likes to scare the wits out of everyone. Problems arise when he has a confrontation with Roxy, a crafty little witch.

When Bruce was eating he was no problem. But when he felt frisky, look out!	Bruce tumbled rocks down the hills and sent the animals off in a panic.	Bruce pushed a rock and it almost landed on Roxy the witch and her cat.
Roxy made a pie that had a magic spell in it. She put it out for Bruce to find and eat.	Bruce ate the pie and shrunk down to the size of a chipmunk.	All the animals chased him and he ended up in a creek. Roxy saved him.

Literature Extensions

Any of Bill Peet's books are excellent resources to use when working with summarization. The books are not too long. Most of them have very distinct events with details that follow.

Students can complete the reproducible found on page 96 using any Bill Peet book. If there are not enough boxes, and/or the boxes are too small for students, then large construction paper can be folded and used instead.

Using Any Book

Storyboards are great ways to help students with summarizing, especially for those students who have a difficult time with writing.

Using a paper bag, students can summarize their book by illustrating and/or writing on each side of the bag. The bag has four sides and a bottom, so a book could be summarized in five parts.

The two large sides of the bag could be split in half, therefore giving students seven areas in which to summarize their book.

Paper-bag storyboards can also be used to help students summarize their reading assignments. This is good for students who have difficulty handling chapter books because they forget what happened in the beginning, or because there are too many pieces of information to put together.

Using a hole punch and brads, have students attach some sheets of paper to the paper bag. The bag can be cut to fit small sheets of construction paper 8½" x 11", or left alone to fit the larger construction paper, 8½" x 22". See diagram below.

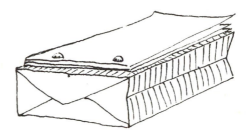

As students complete their reading assignment, have them summarize what they read through illustrations and/or text. The next day, before the student begins reading, have him/her review the storyboard to see what has happened so far. This helps students organize themselves before reading.

Name: _____

Title and author's name: _____

Beginning

Ending

Part IV
Including the
Struggling Learner

The Importance of Flexible Grouping

Part I, "Teaching Through Meaningful Contexts," gives suggestions and ideas to use where there is a wide range of abilities within your classroom. This part gives more specifics about reading materials, assignments, and management of classrooms that have students working at various levels of ability.

One of our goals as teachers is to help students become proficient readers and writers. Sometimes this becomes a vicious cycle with our less proficient readers and writers. They find these tasks difficult to do, and so avoid doing them.

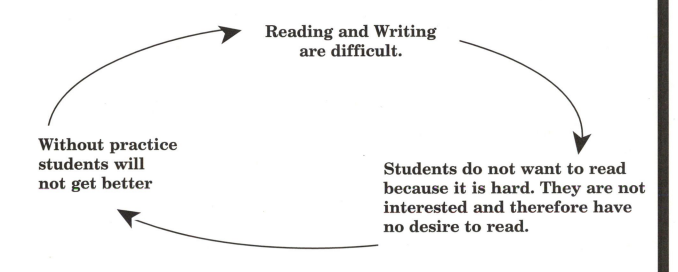

Reading and Writing are difficult.

Students do not want to read because it is hard. They are not interested and therefore have no desire to read.

Without practice students will not get better

The first thing we need to do for these students is to instill a love of reading and writing. They need to see that we value all kinds of books and reading materials, not just "grade-level" materials. (See also "Creating A Print Rich Environment," pages 7–10, for ideas.)

For some students, grade-level materials are where their interest level lies. Yet their ability to actually read those materials may lie significantly below grade level. It is important that both of these areas be addressed in order to ensure that students are motivated and excited about reading (interest level) and, at the same time, are working on their specific reading skills (instructional level).

When students are placed in reading groups solely according to ability, very often they stay there "for life." The groups become stagnant, rarely changing membership. Lower-performing students do not get a chance to interact with higher-performing peers and vice-versa.

The interest level of students is not addressed in this kind of grouping scenario. Reading ability, is addressed on a daily basis, but to the exclusion of interest and motivation.

To solve this, I have used a variety of grouping situations:

whole group
small group
pairs and/or individual reading

Whole-Group Instruction

There needs to be a time each month when students can all share a book. Whole-group instruction is extremely effective and efficient when tasks do not require include fluent reading. These tasks can include:

> preteaching of new concepts and vocabulary
> eliciting prior knowledge
> predicting
> discussing, sharing, giving opinions and other points of view
> debating
> setting purposes for reading and assignments
> modeling fluent reading through reading aloud

Students begin to appreciate each others' points of view. Discussions are truly livelier, richer and more interesting. Positive self-images begin to develop as students see themselves as part of a group, regardless of their reading difficulties.

How does the actual reading get completed? A number of different strategies can be used. If home is an option in terms of supporting and helping students, the Home and School Reading Contract shown here can be used. (A reproducible is provided on the page 101.) Students are responsible for filling in assignments each day.

Home and School Reading Contract

These are reading assignments that the student must do independently, with little or no help. These are books that the student can read with 95% accuracy in comprehension (independent reading level).

Student writes down the reading assignment.

Student puts his/her initials in the box when assignment is complete.

These are reading assignments that have been given during the whole-class reading instruction. These are books that the child cannot read independently, yet he/she can comprehend it when it is read aloud.

Student writes down the reading assignment.

After the parent reads the assigment to the child, the child initials the box.

	Independent	Read Aloud
Monday	☐	☐
Tuesday	☐	☐
Wednesday	☐	☐
Thursday	Pgs. 17-20 ☐	Pgs. 21-28 ☐
Friday	☐	☐
Saturday	☐	☐
Sunday	☐	☐

Home and School Reading Contract

	Independent	Read Aloud
Monday	☐	☐
Tuesday	☐	☐
Wednesday	☐	☐
Thursday	☐	☐
Friday	☐	☐
Saturday	☐	☐
Sunday	☐	☐

The student may have a primer-level book assigned for his or her independent reading and a fifth-grade-level book for the read-aloud. By doing this, both reading level and interest level are addressed.

If home is not an option in terms of supporting the child in his reading development, there are other strategies. These include:

> Reading aloud during whole-group time
> Students reading with a partner
> Listening to the book on tape
> Support personnel reading with the student
> Using a combination of any of these options

Involve students in many different writing activities about books they are reading. Below is a sample of writing that a fourth-grade student completed during independent worktime. The student is reading at a primer level, yet is actively involved in the reading and discussion of the book, *Fantastic Mr. Fox,* by Roald Dahl, during a whole-class format.

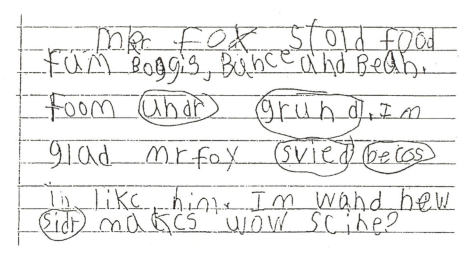

[Mr. Fox stole food from Boggis, Bunce and Bean from underground. I'm glad he survived because I like him. I wonder how cider makes you skinny?]

Small Group

Small groups are used in a variety of different ways. They can be needs-based groups, which bring together students who are having difficulty with the same concept, or who need some enrichment and extension. At times, this can appear to be traditional ability grouping; but it's the need for instruction in certain concepts and skills that brings students together, not necessarily the reading ability.

For example, one of my needs-based groups consisted of students reading from the first-grade level through the fifth-grade level. When writing about the books they read, they all gave very general statements, like "It was great!" "The best book I ever read." "It was awesome!", etc., without backing up those statements with specifics. It didn't matter whether they were discussing *Goldilocks and the Three Bears* or *Call It Courage,* they were all having problems with giving evidence from the book to support their opinions.

Small groups can also be formed when a group of students with the same interests comes together. One way of using small groups with themes is to have a selection of books that deal with survival, for instance, and have students choose what books they want to read. I usually have students select their choices privately on a piece of paper. There are always books of varying degrees of difficulty available.

At times, a student will choose a book that is extremely easy and not challenging at all. If appropriate, the child can also independently read another, more challenging book which deals with the same theme, while still being involved in the group of his choice.

If a child chooses a book that is too difficult, then use some of the suggestions found on page 102 to help him deal successfully with the text. Keep in mind that one of our goals for students is to instill a love and motivation for reading. If a student really wants to read a book that is very challenging, then we need to make it accessible to that child. In doing so, we help to build that self-esteem and motivation which is so important in creating life-long successful readers.

Pairs or Individual Reading

Each month, students read new books, either independently or in pairs. During this time we are usually reviewing skills that have already been taught. For example, during the previous month the class may have chosen the book *Stone Fox* to read as a whole-class novel, and completed the character development activities on pages 50 and 52 of this book. Now, as they read different books, we can review what was learned about character development in *Stone Fox* and apply these lessons to their current books, regardless of whether these books are at a first-grade or sixth-grade level.

During the independent worktime students are usually doing the activities found in "Using Any Book." Also during this time students are involved with many different kinds of literature responses and vocabulary development.

Below are two samples of literature responses which students created during a week of independent and/or paired reading. The first sample is written by a fourth-grade student who is reading at a first-grade level. He is reading the book *Black Beauty*, an *I Can Read* book. He writes:

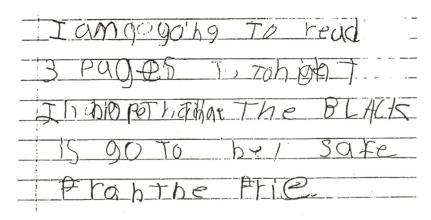

[I am going to read 3 pages tonight. I hope that the black is going to be safe from the fire.]

In the same fourth grade classroom is a child who is reading well above grade level. She writes:

> The Book I'm reading is
> On The Far Side Of The
> Mountain by Jean Craighead
> George. I'm on page 106
> tonight I will read to page
> 116.
>
> I feel bad for Sam, If
> Frightful being confiscated is
> not enough, his sister
> Alice has left the Mountain
> She left with her pig
> Crystal. Crystal has made it
> eayser to track Alice.
> Sam is going to ask a farmer
> if he has seen Alice.
> I hope Sam can find her.
> I don't think Sam is
> thinking about Frightful as
> much now that Alice
> is gone. Maybe it is
> good that Alice left for
> that reason.

[The book I am reading is On the Far Side of the Mountain *by Jean Craighead George. I'm on page 106. tonight. I will read to page 116.*

I feel bad for Sam. If Frightful being confiscated is not enough, his sister Alice has left the mountain. She left with her pig Crystal. Crystal has made it easier to track Alice. Sam is going to ask a farmer if he has seen Alice. I hope Sam can find her.

I don't think Sam is thinking about Frightful as much now that Alice is gone. Maybe it is good that Alice left for that reason.]

Many of the books and activities presented in *Making the Connection: Learning Skills Through Literature (K-2)* are very appropriate for the older, struggling reader. There are open-ended activities and reproducibles that older students can apply to their books.

Books for Struggling Learners

The **Step into Reading** books published by Random House in New York are excellent resources for older students who are struggling with reading. These books are divided into four steps, Step 1 being the easiest and Step 4 the most difficult. Listed below is a sampling of the books available. While there are many other titles, I've listed the ones my students have suggested.

Step 2 Books

Christopher Columbus

Dolphins

Dinosaur Days

Hungry, Hungry Sharks

The Bravest Dog Ever: The True Story of Bolto

The Pied Piper of Hamelin

Whales: The Gentle Giants

Wild, Wild Wolves

Step 3 Books

Amazing Rescues

Pompeii: Buried Alive

Space Rock

The Titanic: Lost and Found

Step 4 Books

A Wall Of Names: The Story of the Vietnam Veterans Memorial

Barry: The Bravest Saint Bernard

Baseball's Best

Comeback

Dinosaur Hunters

Jackie Robinson and the Story of All-Black Baseball

Moonwalk

The Trojan Horse: How the Greeks Won the War

True-Life Treasure Hunts

Who Shot the President? The Death of John F. Kennedy

Bullseye Step Into Classics, also published by Random House in New York, are books that my students have had success with and enjoyed. They include:

Black Beauty
Knights of the Round Table
Robin Hood
The Secret Garden
Treasure Island
The Hunchback of Notre Dame
Kidnapped
The Time Machine

Bullseye Chillers include:
Frankenstein
The Mummy Awakes
The Phantom of the Opera
Return of the Werewolf
Dr. Jekyll and Mr. Hyde

Harper Trophy has a series entitled **An I Can Read Book.** There are three levels in this series. I recommend the third level, which states on the books, "grades 2–4." Most of the books in this level are historical fiction and of high interest. Some titles include:

George the Drummer Boy
Sam the Minuteman
The Drinking Gourd
Dolphin
The Boston Tea Party
Egg to Chick
The Long Way Westward

Scholastic has a series entitled **Hello Reader**, which comes in four levels. Level four states on the book "grades 2 & 3". The fiction books at this level were not of high interest to my older students; however, the nonfiction books at this level were great. Some titles include:

Wild Weather: Tornadoes
Wild Weather: Hurricanes
Finding the Titanic
Armies of Ants
Dancing With Manatees
Great Black Heroes: Five Brave Explorers
Great Black Heroes: Five Notable Inventors

Little, Brown and Company have a series written by Matt Christopher. These are novels that deal with sports.

Big Books are also excellent resources to use with older students. (See page 79 for ideas about using the big book *The Great Gray Owl* with students.) Scholastic books have a Big Book science series called Big Science. Each Big Book revolves around a specific science topic. Some topics include:

> Stormy Weather
> Matter
> Earth Forces
> Plants
> Animal Homes
> Solar System

One of the ways to motivate students, and really get them hooked on reading, is to have these books available to everyone. Many times it is the extremely proficient student who reads these suggested books because of their topics and interest level. In turn, the less proficient reader, who really needs to be reading the most but is not interested because of his ability, becomes motivated and excited.

Traveling Through Literature: A Culminating Activity

"Traveling Through Literature" was a collaborative project between twelve fourth- and fifth-grade classrooms in one school district. Teachers wanted to do something to bring the different schools in the district together and, at the same time, get students excited about reading.

Some of the teachers had been to a workshop presented by Caren Honigfeld and Rose-Marie Botting of Fort Lauderdale, Florida. Ms. Honigfeld and Ms. Botting told us about a bubble that could be made from plastic, where students could actually go inside of it. We took this bubble concept and came up with the idea of making literature bubbles.

Each classroom was responsible for choosing a novel and bringing it alive by creating a world inside a plastic bubble. Bubbles were made with rolls of plastic.

We made an assembly line one afternoon in the gym. All of the plastic was cut and put together.

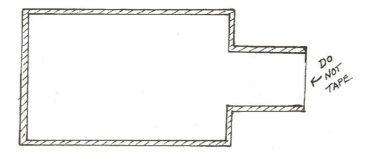

The plastic was cut into the above shape. Two pieces were laid on top of each other. All of the sides, except one end, were taped closed with duct tape.

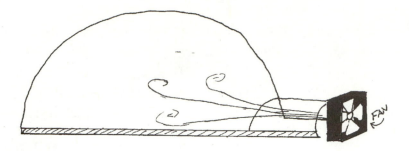

An electric fan was placed at the untaped end. When the fan was turned on, the plastic bubble blew up.

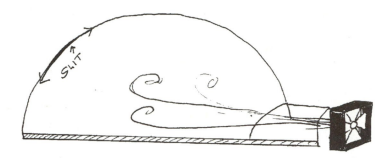

Now a slit needed to be made in order for students to enter the balloon. Each classroom was responsible for making a bubble. The ideas students came up with were incredible!

This is the bubble created for *Twenty-One Balloons*, by William deBois.

This bubble represents the book, *The Lion, the Witch, and the Wardrobe*. Note the wardrobe that students need to go through in order to enter the bubble.

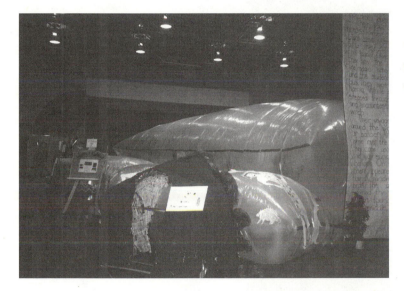

This is the outside of the bubble to *My Side of the Mountain*, by Jean Craighead George.

Inside the bubble, students met Matt.

This is the bubble that represents the book, *The Magic School Bus: Lost in the Solar System*.

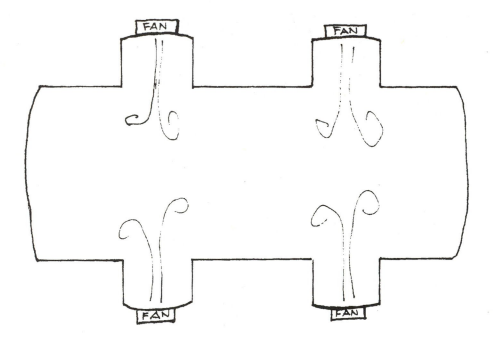

One huge bubble was made that stretched across the whole gymnasium. It was cut out in the above shape to allow for four fans to blow it up.

This is how the bubbles were set up for the program. Students began in the big bubble, and then went in groups to one of the little bubbles. In the photo, each group of students is at one of the literature worlds. Every ten minutes, music was played, and the students then rotated to the next bubble.

Each class was responsible for making a poster that contained:

the name of their book

a class picture

a picture representing something in the book

They were all displayed
in the large bubble.

The Conway Daily Sun

FRIDAY, MAY 27, 1994   VOL. 6 NO. 107   CONWAY, NH   MT. WASHINGTON VALLEY'S DAILY NEWSPAPER   356-2999   **FREE**

Bubbles bring together students from all five elementary schools

By Lloyd Jones
THE CONWAY DAILY SUN

BARTLETT — The banner hanging from the rafters at Bartlett Elementary School summed up the day best for the fourth and fifth grade students in SAU 9.

"Once upon a time in the beautiful valley of the Saco, 12 fourth and fifth grades decided to begin an incredible journey.

"Their journey took them across *Troubled River*, into *Giant Land*, where they met the *B.F.G.* They continued on to the *Planet Owlstonia Crown*. *The Magic School Bus* arrived and the students boarded the bus. They were on their way to *Narnia*. While in Narnia they stepped through a wardrobe and encountered a *Lion and a Witch*.

"Their voyage continued around the world in a hot air balloon and all of a sudden while over the Atlantic Ocean, they came upon a platform that was supported by *twenty-one balloons*. On the far horizon there appeared a *giant peach* flown by hundreds of white birds. The giant peach rammed the balloon and the children found themselves in the middle of a scorching desert. Their *Deathwatch* had begun. They wished and wished and wished. Before their eyes appeared a *Wishgiver* who took them to the coolness of the *Winter Room*. They sat together and heard wonderful tales such as *My Side of the Mountain* and *The Banner in the Sky*.

"Their journey brought them to the Bartlett Elementary School where their incredible adventures continued through their love of literature."

More than 220 fourth and fifth graders from Jackson Grammar, Conway Elementary, Pine Tree, John Fuller and Bartlett Elementary School participated together, all at once, for the first time. The program, entitled "Traveling Through Literature," brought the students together for an activity that involved math, science, social studies and literature skills. Each class, there were 12 in all, presented a demonstration on a certain theme from a book they have been studying.

Now the neat thing — everything was done in student-made and decorated bubbles. Each class had its own bubble, which was assembled with plastic sheeting, like tarp, some tape and a fan. Combining the three the students created biosphere bubbles.

"It turned out much better than I ever thought was possible," Harry Benson, SAU 9 superintendent, said. "I knew the creativity and all the time and effort that went into the planning, but this was far more than I ever expected. The teachers, parents and students put together something that really is something to be proud of . . . I'm sure that this is something that the kids will always remember."

The bubbles program took months of planning by a district-wide PIMMS (Program Improving Mastering in Math and Science) committee, which tossed around numerous ideas before settling on the bubbles program in December. From that point forward each of the participating classes began working on their bubble presentations, preparing for Wednesday.

Jackson Principal Steve Bamsey said he hopes there will be further projects that will bring all of the classes together. Students from Jackson set their bubble up around the book "The Winter Room." Each group of students who visited the bubble was divided in half. Seven went into the bubble for a demonstration while the remaining seven stayed outside for another program. After four minutes the two groups swapped places. Every eight minutes, each of the groups rotated to another station.

"Out here we have a tape recorder with an excerpt from the book on it," Bamsey said. "Our presentation on the inside talks about the entire book."

Bamsey was impressed at how smoothly the day flowed. "Pat Pavelka and Peg Fish are the brains behind this entire project," he said. "They took control, organized it and deserve all the credit as far as physical structuring goes . . . Hopefully, we can do this kind of sharing project again whether it be in science, math or music. It's just exciting to be a part of."

Pavelka said her chief concern heading into the project was the number of students participating, but it was never a problem. "Everyone was just so attentive," she said. "I've had a couple of students come up to me and say that they can't wait to go back and read this or that book.

"My hope is that the kids will be turned onto books after this," Pavelka said. "The cooperative learning that took place was exceptional."

Fish echoed similar sentiments. "The kids have been phenomenal," she said. "The cooperation of everyone has been unbelievable. You wouldn't believe there were 200 students in here unless someone told you . . . This has been something the kids have been looking forward to for a while. They look forward to mixing just like the teachers look forward to brainstorming.

Sarah Wentworth, a student at Conway Elementary, summed up the program the best. "It's cool," she said. Her favorite part? "The bubbles and all the neat stories. I hope we get to do something like this again."

Bibliography

Bibliography of Children's Literature

These children's books have been categorized into the following genres:

      History/Social Studies
      Traditional
      Fiction
      Mysteries
      Fantasy
      Multicultural
      Picture Books
      Poems

Keep in mind, as you read through the lists, that some of these books could fit into more than one category.

History/Social Studies

Aliki. *A Weed is a Flower: The Life of George Washington Carver.* New York: Aladdin, 1988.

Armstrong, William. *Sounder.* New York: Harper Trophy, 1969.

Bulla, Clyde Robert. *Squanto: Friend of the Pilgrims.* New York: Scholastic, 1954.

Cohen, Barbara. *Molly's Pilgrim.* New York: Bantam Skylark, 1983.

Conrad, Pam. *Pedro's Journal.* New York: Scholastic, 1991.

D'Aulaire. *Columbus.* New York, NY: Doubleday.

Dalgliesh, Alice. *The Courage of Sarah Noble.* New York: Aladdin Books, 1954.

Denenberg, Barry. *When Will This Cruel War Be Over?* New York: Scholastic, 1996.

Fritz, Jeane. *And Then What Happened, Paul Revere?* New York: Putnam & Grosset, 1996.

———. *Can't You Make Them Behave, King George?* New York: Putnam & Grosset, 1985.

———. *Shh! We're Writing the Constitution.* New York: Putnam & Grosset, 1987.

———. *What's the Big Idea, Ben Franklin?* New York: Coward, McCann & Geoghegan, 1976.

Gregory, Kristiana. *The Winter of Red Snow.* New York: Scholastic, 1996.

Lasky, Kathryn. *A Journey to the New World.* New York: Scholastic, 1996.

Lowry, Lois. *Number the Stars.* New York: Dell Yearling, 1989.

MacLachlan, Patricia. *Sarah, Plain and Tall.* New York: HarperCollins, 1985.

McGovern, Ann. *Wanted Dead or Alive: The True Story of Harriet Tubman.* New York: Scholastic, 1977.

Monio, F.N. *The Drinking Gourd.* New York: HarperCollins, 1970.

O'Dell, Scott. *Island of the Blue Dolphins.* New York: Dell Publishing, 1960.

Sook, Nyul Chol. *Year of Impossible Good Byes*. New York: Bantam Doubleday, 1991.

Speare, Elizabeth George. *The Sign of the Beaver*. New York: Dell Publishing, 1983.

————. *The Witch of Blackbird Pond*. South Holland, IL: Dell Yearling, 1972.

Sterling, Dorothy. *Freedom Train: The Story of Harriet Tubman* . New York: Scholastic, 1987.

Taylor, Theodore. *The Cay*. New York: Avon Books, 1969.

Waters, Kate. *Sarah Morton's Day: a Day in the Life of a Pilgrim Girl*. New York: Scholastic, 1993.

Wilder, Laura Ingalls. *The Little House Books (Series)*. New York: Harper Trophy.

————. The American Girls Collection (Series). Middletown, WI: Pleasant Company.

Traditional

Bishop, Claire Huchet, and Kurt Wiese. *The Five Chinese Brothers*. New York: Putnam & Grosset, 1989.

Climo, Shirley. *The Egyptian Cinderella*. New York: Crowel, 1989.

Gross, Gwen. *Knights of the Round Table*. New York: Random House, 1985.

Heyer, Carol. *Excalibur*. Nashville, TN: Ideals Children's Books, 1991.

Kipling, Rudyard. *The Elephant's Child*. Orlando, FL: Harcourt Brace, 1983.

Lester, Julius. *John Henry*. New York: Dial Books, 1994.

Louie, Ai-Ling. *Yeh-Shen*. New York: Philomel, 1982.

Pyle, Howard. *King Arthur*. Mahwah, NJ: Troll Associates, 1988.

Steptoe, John. *Mufaro's Beautiful Daughters*. New York: Scholastic, 1987.

Young, Ed. *Lon Po Po: A Red Riding Hood Story From China*. New York: Philomel, 1990.

————. *The Legend of Sleepy Hollow* (adapted from the original by Washington Irving). Nashvllle, TN: Ideals Children's Books, 1991.

Traditional With a Modern Twist

Lowell, Susan. *The Three Little Javelinas*. Flagstaff, AZ: Northland, 1992.

Minters, Frances. *Sleepless Beauty*. New York: Viking, 1996.

Scieszka, Jon. *Knights of the Kitchen Table*. New York: Puffin Books, 1991.

————. *The True Story of the Three Little Pigs*. New York: Viking, 1989.

Scieszka, Jon and Johnson, Steve. *The Frog Prince, Continued*. New York: Viking, 1991.

Trivizas, Eugene & Oxenbury, Helen. *The Three Little Wolves and the Big Bad Pig*. New York: Macmillan, 1993.

Zipes, Jack (Editor). *The Outspoken Princess & the Gentle Knight*. New York: Bantam Books, 1994.

Fiction

Bauer, Marion Dane. *On My Honor*. New York: Dell Yearling, 1986.

Blume, Judy. *Superfudge*. New York: Dell Yearling, 1980.

———. *Tales of a Fourth Grade Nothing*. New York: Dell Yearling, 1972.

Boyd, Candy Dawson. *Circle of Gold*. New York: Scholastic, 1984.

———. *Forever Friends*. New York: Puffin, 1985.

Byars, Betsy. *The Pinballs*. New York: HarperCollins, 1977.

———. *Trouble River*. New York: Scholastic, 1969.

Cleary, Beverly. *Muggi E Maggi E*. New York: Avon Books, 1990.

———. *Ramona and Her Mother*. South Holland, IL: Dell Yearling, 1984.

———. *Ramona Forever*. South Holland, IL: Dell Yearling, 1979.

———. *Ramona the Brave*. South Holland, IL: Dell Yearling, 1975.

———. *Strider*. New York: Avon Books, 1991.

Dahl, Roald. *Danny the Champion of the World*. New York: Puffin, 1975.

DeClements, Barthe. *Nothing's Fair in Fifth Grade*. New York: Puffin, 1981.

———. *Sixth Grade Can Really Kill You*. New York: Puffin, 1985.

———. *The Fourth Grade Wizards*. New York: Puffin, 1988.

Easley, MaryAnn. *I Am the Ice Worm*. Honesdale, PA: Boyds Mills, 1996.

George, Jean Craighead. *My Side of the Mountain*. New York: Puffin, 1991.

———. *On the Far Side of the Mountain*. New York: Puffin, 1990.

London, Jack. *The Call of the Wild*. Stamford, CT: Longmeadow Press, 1994.

———. *White Fang*. Stamford, CT: Longmeadow Press, 1994.

Naylor, Phyllis Reynolds. *Shiloh*. New York: Dell Yearling, 1991.

Park, Barbara. *Almost Starring Skinnybones*. New York: Bullseye Book, 1982.

———. *Skinnybones*. New York: Bullseye Book, 1982.

———. *The Kid in the Red Jacket*. New York: Bullseye Book, 1987.

Paterson, Katherine. *Bridge to Terabithia*. New York: Avon Books, 1977.

———. *Lyddie*. New York: Puffin, 1991.

———. *Park's Quest*. New York: Puffin, 1988.

Paulsen, Gary. *Canyons*. New York: Dell Publishing, 1990.

———. *Dogsong*. New York: Puffin, 1987.

———. *Hatchet*. New York: Puffin, 1987.

———. *The River*. New York: Dell Yearling, 1991.

———. *The Winter Room*. New York: Dell Yearling, 1989.

———. *Tracker*. New York: Scholastic, 1984.

———. *Woodsong*. New York: Puffin Book, 1990.

Rawls, Wilson. *Where the Red Fern Grows*. New York: Bantam Doubleday, 1961.

Roth, Arthur. *Avalanche*. New York: Scholastic, 1979.

Sachar, Louis. *Sideways Stories From Wayside School*. New York: Avon Books, 1978.

———. *There's a Boy in the Girl's Bathroom*. New York: Randam House, 1987.

————. *Wayside School Is Falling Down.* New York: Avon Books, 1989.

Smith, Doris Buchanan. *A Taste of Blackberries.* New York: HarperTrophy, 1973.

Spinell, Jerry. *Maniac Magee.* New York: HarperCollins, 1990.

Ullman, James Ramsey. *Banner in the Sky.* New York: Scholastic, 1982.

Warner, Gertrude Chandler. *The Boxcar Children Series.* Niles, IL: Albert Whitman & Co., 1977.

White, Robb. *Deathwatch.* New York: Dell Publishing, 1972.

Mysteries

Adler, David A. *Cam Jansen Series.* New York: Scholastic, 1980.

Dixon, Franklin W. *Hardy Boys Mysteries.* New York: Simon & Schuster.

George, Jean Craighead. *Who Really Killed Cock Robin?* New York: Penguin, 1984.

Herzig, Allison Cragin, and Jane Lawrence Mali. *Mystery on October Road.* Scholastic, 1991.

Keene, Carolyn. *Nancy Drew Mysteries.* New York: Grosset & Dunlap.

Sharmat, Marjorie Weinman. *Nate the Great Series.* New York: Dell Yearling.

Sobol, Donald J. *Encyclopedia Brown Boy Detective Series.* New York: Bantam.

Fantasy

Atwater, Richard & Florence Atwater. *Mr. Popper's Penguins.* Boston, MA: Little, Brown & Co., 1966.

Banks, Lynne Reid. *The Indian in the Cupboard.* New York: Avon Books, 1980.

————. *The Return of the Indian.* New York: Avon Books, 1986.

————. *The Secret Indian.* New York: Avon Books, 1989.

Dahl, Roald. *Charlie and the Great Glass Elevator.* New York: Puffin, 1972.

————. *James and the Giant Peach.* New York: Puffin, 1961.

————. *Matilda.* New York: Puffin, 1988.

————. *The Witches.* New York: Puffin, 1983.

Howe, James. *Bunnicula: A Rabbit Tale of Mystery.* New York: Avon Books, 1980.

————. *Howliday Inn.* New York: Avon Books, 1982.

————. *The Celery Stalks at Midnight.* New York: Avon Books, 1984.

Peet, Bill. *Chester the Worldly Pig.* Boston, MA: Houghton Mifflin, 1965.

————. *Cowardly Clyde.* Boston, MA: Houghton Mifflin, 1979.

————. *Ella.* Boston, MA: Houghton Mifflin, 1964.

————. *Jennifer and Josephine.* Boston, MA: Houghton Mifflin, 1967.

————. *No Such Things.* Boston, MA: Houghton Mifflin, 1983.

————. *Pamela Camel.* Boston, MA: Houghton Mifflin, 1984.

Selden, George. *The Cricket in Times Square.* New York: Bantam Doubleday, 1960.

Van Allsburg, Chris. *Jumanji.* Boston, MA: Houghton Mifflin, 1981.

———. *The Polar Express.* Boston, MA: Houghton Mifflin, 1985.

———. *The Widow's Broom.* Boston, MA: Houghton Mifflin, 1992.

———. *The Wreck of the Zephyr.* Boston, MA: Houghton Mifflin, 1983.

White, E.B. *Charlotte's Web.* New York: Harper Trophy, 1980.

———. *Stuart Little.* New York: Harper Trophy, 1973.

Multicultural

Bell, Sharon. *The Hundred Penny Box.* New York: Viking Penguin, 1975.

DeSpain, Pleasant. *Thirty-Three Multicultural Tales to Tell.* Little Rock, AR: August House, 1993.

Feelings, Muriel. *Jambo Means Hello: Swahili Alphabet Book.* New York: Puffin Pied Piper, 1981.

Goble, Paul. *Girl Who Loved Wild Horses.* New York: Aladdin, 1978.

———. *The Gift of the Sacred Dog.* New York: Aladdin, 1980.

———. *The Great Race of the Birds & Animals.* New York: Aladdin, 1985.

Martin, Bill. *Knots on a Counting Rope.* New York: Holt & Co., 1987.

McDermott, Gerald. *Arrow to the Sun.* New York: Puffin Books, 1977.

Miles, Miska. *Annie & the Old One.* Boston, MA: Little, Brown & Co., 1971.

Musgrove, Margaret. *Ashanti to Zulu: African Traditions.* New York: Pied Piper Printing, 1980.

Paterson, Katherine. *The Tale of the Mandarin Ducks.* Lodestar, 1990.

Sperry, Armstrong. *Call It Courage.* New York: Aladdin, 1990.

Taylor, Mildred D. *Song of the Trees.* New York: Bantam Skylark, 1975.

———. *The Friendship and the Gold Cadillac.* Bantam Skylark, 1987.

Ward, Lella. *I Am Eyes Ni Macho.* New York: Scholastic, 1987.

Picture Books

Baker, J. *Where the Forest Meets the Sea.* New York: Scholastic, 1987.

Berger, B. *Grandfather Twilight.* New York: Philomel, 1984.

Blazek, Sarah Kirwan. *An Irish Night Before Christmas.* Gretna, LA: Pelican, 1996.

Cannon, Janell. *Stellaluna.* New York: Harcourt Brace, 1993.

Cherry, Lynne. *A River Ran Wild.* New York: Gulliver Green Books, 1992.

———. *The Armadillo From Amarillo.* New York: Gulliver Green Books, 1994.

———. *The Great Kapok Tree.* New York: Gulliver Green Books, 1990.

Cochrane, Orin. *The Great Gray Owl.* Steinbach, Manitoba: Derksen Printers, 1986.

Edens, Cooper. *Santa Cows.* New York: Simon & Schuster, 1991.

Fox, Mem. *Wilfrid Gordon McDonald Partridge.* New York: Kane/Miller, 1985.

Gwynne, Fred. *A Chocolate Moose for Dinner.* New York: Treehouse, 1976.

———. *A Little Pigeon Toad.* New York: Treehouse, 1988.

The King Who Rained. New York: Prentice-Hall, 1970.

———. *The Sixteen-Hand Horse.* New York: Treehouse, 1987.

Heller, Ruth. *A Cache of Jewels.* New York: Grosset & Dunlap, 1987.

———. *Kites Sail High.* New York: Grosset & Dunlap, 1988.

———. *Many Luscious Lollipops.* New York: Putnam & Grosset, 1989.

———. *Merry-Go-Round.* New York: Grosset & Dunlap, 1990.

Hepworth, Cathi. *Antics!* New York: G.P. Putnam's Sons, 1992.

Hoban, Tana. *Look! Look! Look!* New York: Scholastic, 1988.

Innocenti, R. *Rose Blanche.* Markato, MN: Creative Education, 1985.

Jacobs, Howard (Editor). *Cajun Night Before Christmas.* Gretna, LA: Pelican, 1992.

Most, Bernard. *There's an Ant in Anthony.* New York: Mulberry, 1980.

Pallotta, Jerry. *The Flower Alphabet Book.* Watertown, MA: Charlesbridge Publishing, 1988.

———. *The Frog Alphabet Book.* Watertown, MA: Charlesbridge Publishing, 1990.

———. *The Ocean Alphabet Book.* Watertown, MA: Charlesbridge Publishing, 1986.

Pallotta, Jerry & Thomson, Bob. *The Victory Garden Alphabet Book.* Watertown, MA: Charlesbridge Publishing, 1992.

Parish, Peggy. *Good Work, Amelia Bedelia.* New York: Avon Books, 1976.

Sheldon, Dyan. *The Whale's Song.* New York: Dial Books, 1991.

Spiers, P. *People.* New York: Doubleday, 1980.

Tsuchiya, Y. *Faithful Elephants.* Boston, MA: Houghton Mifflin, 1988.

Van Allsburg, Chris. *Just a Dream.* Boston, MA: Houghton Mifflin, 1990.

———. *The Mysteries of Harris Burdick.* Boston, MA: Houghton Mifflin, 1984.

Wood, Audrey. *Quick As a Cricket.* Singapore: Child's Play, 1982.

Poems

Bennett, George and Paul Molloy (Editors). *Cavalcade of Poems.* New York: Scholastic, 1968.

Burns, Marjorie (Editor). *A Handful of Haiku.* New York: Scholastic, 1990.

Demi (Editor). *In the Eyes of the Cat: Japanese Poetry for All Seasons.* New York: Henry Holt, 1992.

Molloy, Paul (Editor). *Poetry U.S.A.* New York: Scholastic, 1968.

O'Neill, Mary. *Hailstones and Halibut Bones.* New York: Doubleday, 1961.

Prelutsky, Jack. *A Pizza the Size of the Sun.* New York: Greenwillow Books, 1996.

———. *The Dragons Are Singing Tonight.* New York: Greenwillow Books, 1993.

Sears, Peter. *Gonna Bake Me a Rainbow Poem.* New York: Scholastic, 1990.

Silverstein, Shel. *Where the Sidewalk Ends.* New York: Harper & Row, 1974.

Soto, Gary. *A Fire in My Hands.* New York: Scholastic, 1990.

Yolen, Jane (Selected by). *Mother Earth Father Sky.* Honesdale, PA: Boyds Mills Press, 1996.

Professional Bibliography

Atwell, Nancie. *Coming to Know: Writing to Learn in the Intermediate Grades.* Portsmouth, NH: Heinemann, 1990.

————. *Side By Side.* Portsmouth, NH: Heinemann, 1991.

————. *In the Middle: Writing, Reading and Learning With Adolescents.* Portsmouth, NH: Heinemann, 1987.

Calkins, Lucy. *Living Between the Lines.* Portsmouth, NH: Heinemann, 1991.

————. *The Art of Teaching Writing.* Portsmouth, NH: Heinemann, 1986.

Cordeiro, Pat. *Whole Learning: Whole Language and Content in the Upper Elementary Grades.* Katonah, NY: Richard C. Owen Publishers, Inc.

Daniels, Harvey. *Literature Circles: Voice and Choice in the Student-Centered Classroom.* York, ME: Stenhouse Publishers, 1994.

Fletcher, Ralph. *What a Writer Needs.* Portsmouth, NH: Heinemann, 1993.

Forester, Anne D. and Margaret Reinhard. *The Teacher's Way.* Winnipeg, Manitoba: Peguis Publishers, 1994.

————. *On the Move: Teaching the Learners' Way in Grades 4-7.* Winnipeg, Manitoba, Peguis Publishers, 1991.

Gentry, J. Richard, and Jean Wallace Gillet. *Teaching Kids to Spell.* Portsmouth, NH: Heinemann, 1993.

Graves, Donald H. *A Fresh Look at Writing.* Portsmouth, NH: Heinemann, 1994.

————. *Build a Literate Classroom.* Portsmouth, NH: Heinemann, 1991.

————. *Experiment With Fiction.* Portsmouth, NH: Heinemann, 1991.

————. *Explore Poetry.* Portsmouth, NH: Heinemann, 1992.

————. *Investigate Nonfiction.* Portsmouth, NH: Heinemann, 1989.

Harste, Jerome and Kathy Short. *Creating Classrooms for Authors.* Portsmouth, NH: Heinemann, 1993.

Lane, Barry. *After the End.* Portsmouth, NH: Heinemann, 1993.

Moss, Joy. *Using Literature in the Middle Grades: A Thematic Approach.* Norwood, MA: Christopher-Gordon Publishers, Inc., 1994.

Pace, Glennellen (Editor). *Whole Learning in the Middle School: Evolution and Transition.* Norwood, MA: Christopher-Gordon Publishers, Inc.

Routman, Regie. *Invitations.* Portsmouth, NH: Heinemann, 1991.

Trelease, Jim. *The New Read-Aloud Handbook.* New York, New York: Penguin Books, 1989.

Wells, Jan and Linda Hart-Hewins. *Read It in the Classroom! Organizing an Interactive Language Arts Program Grades 4-9.* Portsmouth, NH: Heinemann, 1992.

Index

Index of Children's Literature and Children's Authors